Wake Up, Counselors!

Restoring Counseling Services for Troubled Teens

William L. Fibkins

ROWMAN & LITTLEFIELD EDUCATION
A division of
ROWMAN & LITTLEFIELD PUBLISHERS, INC.
Lanham • New York • Toronto • Plymouth, UK

Published by Rowman & Littlefield Education
A division of Rowman & Littlefield Publishers, Inc.
A wholly owned subsidiary of The Rowman & Littlefield Publishing Group, Inc.
4501 Forbes Boulevard, Suite 200, Lanham, Maryland 20706
www.rowman.com

10 Thornbury Road, Plymouth PL6 7PP, United Kingdom

British Library Cataloguing in Publication Information Available

Library of Congress Cataloging-in-Publication Data

Fibkins, William L.
Wake up, counselors! : restoring counseling services for troubled teens / William L. Fibkins.
p. cm.
Includes bibliographical references.
ISBN 978-1-61048-818-1 (cloth : alk. paper) -- ISBN 978-1-61048-819-8 (pbk. : alk. paper) -- ISBN
978-1-61048-820-4 (electronic)
1. Counseling in secondary education--United States. 2. School failure--United States--Prevention. 3.
Behavior modification--United States. I. Title.
LB1620.5.F479 2013
371.40973--dc23

2013012116

Table of Contents

Chapter One

The Impact of the Demise of Personal Counseling Services in Our Schools

This book begins with two observations highlighted in the 2011 report "Counseling at the Crossroads."[1] One, it briefly summarizes the development of school counseling in the United States. Secondly, it provides a current view of the school counseling profession and asserts that the role of the school counselor is frequently murky, with poorly defined goals that lack clarity of purpose and prevent counselors from maximizing their impact on the lives of children.

Counselors in today's schools say they are involved in a profession "in search of an identity" and are disenchanted with the quality of both their profession and the schools in which they work.

Here is what the "Counseling at the Crossroads" report has to say about the roots of the profession and where it is today, a profession in crisis. The work suggests that the practice of school counseling began informally in American schools as teachers, administrators, parents, and others gave vocational and life guidance to students. The counseling of youth was established as a widespread presence in our nation's schools with the 1958 National Defense Education Act, which provided funds to train and place counselors in schools across America.

Comprehensive counseling programs that focused on both developmental psychology and educational achievement emerged by the end of the 1980s, and have largely informed current practices in the counseling professions. In 1995, the Education Trust, veering away from the traditional pathways, launched the Transforming School Counseling Initiative, a national effort to reshape school counseling through preservice training of school counselors that focused on equity in student outcomes, creating counselors who could be

1

leaders, advocates, and systemic-change agents, intentionally focusing on
ensuring brighter futures for all students.

By 1998, a need for more consistent and high-quality school counseling
programs led the American School Counselor Association (ASCA) to create
national standards for counselors and counseling programs. Yet while comprehensive counseling programs and the ASCA model, which was developed
in 2005 and included many of the tenets put forth by the Education Trust,
have become commonplace in American schools, confusion and misunderstanding about the proper role and use of school counselors remain part of
the field.

In schools across America today, the day-to-day job of the counselor
includes personal-needs counseling, the choice and scheduling of school
courses, academic testing, postsecondary admission counseling, occupational
counseling and job placement, teaching, and other nonguidance activities
(e.g., new student registration, record maintenance, and other administrative
tasks).

Often, *counselor* is less of a defined position in schools than a catchall:
when schools, teachers, and administrators need a job done, or when new
responsibilities arise, they tend to look to the school counselor. As of 2008
(the most recent data available), more than 130,000 counselors were hard at
work in our nation's schools, with job descriptions as diverse as the students
they serve.

This second section of the "Counseling at the Crossroads" report suggests
that the role of the counselors is frequently murky, with poorly defined goals
that may place them with one foot inside the traditional education system and
the other foot in a network of mental- and social-support services that is not
uniformly tied to the rest of the education system. Counselors report lacking
clarity of purpose both in their day-to-day responsibilities and as a part of the
broader education system.

Despite the increased focus in the United States on academic success and
postsecondary achievement, current state and federal laws pertaining to
school counseling are limited; counselors have remained largely in the background of major school-reform initiatives. In all, much of the confusion and
poor deployment of school counselors across the education system seems to
arise from what has been described as a general lack of understanding by
critical stakeholders about what school counselors do that impacts student
outcomes. This lack of clarity may prevent counselors from maximizing their
impact on the lives of children. School counselors are a vital part of the
education system and play key roles in supporting students in holistic ways.
These professionals, who are often former teachers themselves, are uniquely
positioned to support student achievement, not just because of their specialized education, but because they have a more complete, year-to-year perception of every student they counsel.

The school counseling profession, which began with great expectations and national support in the 1950s, now finds itself mired in an outdated organizational model in which counselors feel their mission is unclear. They see a disturbing gap between what the mission of their profession should be and the reality they are facing in the schools.

This book's intent is to describe how the much-heralded school counseling program lost its purpose and effectiveness and what needs to be done to elevate it once again to being a major source of help for students, parents, school staff, and administrators.

What went wrong and led to the present-day school counselors' disenchantment? A top priority for secondary school public relations and media promotion is stating that their counseling intervention services are at work 24/7 to prevent even one student from falling through the cracks. However, the reality behind this glowing assessment contains a far different story for troubled teens in need of personal counseling.

Providing individual and group counseling for secondary school students was once a major priority for secondary school counselors. However, many guidance programs have abandoned this role, and counselors have become quasi-administrators who spend most of their time scheduling students for classes, managing the mandated testing program, resolving discipline issues, and advising students on college admissions.

Counseling students on personal and well-being issues takes up a very small part of the time. As a result, in many school districts social workers, student-assistance counselors, and school psychologists have taken over the counselors' counseling duties.

However, two critical issues are now causing school leaders to consider reorganizing school guidance staff so there is a cadre of counselors trained and charged with the mission of providing individual and group counseling for troubled teens. First, the number of troubled teens arriving at the schoolhouse door looking for help has exploded. Second, budget cuts have eliminated or drastically curtailed many of the services of social workers, student-assistance counselors, and psychologists. The result? Many open doors for help are now closed and the schools' counseling services are failing many students, parents, and educators in need of intervention.

This book provides a new model in which well-trained counselors can once again regain their historic role in counseling troubled teens and parents and training staff and students on the front lines to act, not look away, when they observe a student heading toward the margins of school life.

Criticism of the way counselors currently deliver their counseling services is on the rise and pushing counselor leaders and secondary school principals to reorganize these services. A new report by Jean Johnson and Jon Rochkind, "Can I Get a Little Advice Here?,"[2] states that most young adults who go to college believe that the advice of their high school guidance counselors was inadequate and often impersonal and perfunctory.

Most troubling for policymakers is that young people characterized their interactions with guidance counselors as "anonymous and unhelpful." Nearly half of those surveyed said their counselors made them feel "like I was just another face in the crowd."

The researchers noted that counselors' responsibilities have only grown in recent years. They also reported that advising students on higher-education choices is just one of the many things that guidance counselors do. Much of their effort is devoted to discipline issues, scheduling students for classes, overseeing mandated testing programs, and other administrative duties.

Jim Jump, a high school counselor and president of the National Association of College Admissions, said in the report that "so many other things are tossed on counselors' plates that actual counseling takes up a very small part of the time."

One of the important conclusions of the study is that young people typically give their teachers and mentors much better ratings than the dismal ratings assigned to counselors. Solid majorities of young adults from diverse ethnic and racial backgrounds report that they had a teacher who really took an interest in them and encouraged them to go to college. Most say they had a teacher or coach who really inspired them and motivated them to do their best.

There is a vicious cycle going on in our large high schools. Many administrators are being inundated with increased responsibilities. Unfortunately they are adding more of these increased responsibilities to the counselors' role, resulting in the diminishing, even elimination, of personal counseling services for students, parents, and at-risk educators. The result? A dramatic increase in at-risk students, parents, and educators seeking help but finding the counselor's door closed.

Far too many leaders in the school counseling profession, including guidance directors, have accepted this diminished role of personal counseling and have not opposed or challenged their administrator's decision to make the guidance and counseling department an extension of the administration. The report by Jean Johnson and Jon Rochkind (cited above) lays bare the results.

The personal counseling role of secondary school counselors is being reduced by the steady increase in noncounseling duties. A new state law in New Jersey, the Anti-Bullying Bill of Rights,[3] demanded that, beginning in September 2011, all public schools adopt anti-bullying policies, increase staff training, and adhere to tight deadlines for reporting incidents. The law requires that a school must designate an anti-bullying specialist to investigate complaints and that each district must have a bullying coordinator.

In most cases schools are tapping guidance counselors as the new anti-bullying specialists, raising the question of whether they have the time to look into every complaint of harassment and write the detailed reports required. This author sees this as one more step in the bureaucratizing of the guidance counselor's role and as further distancing them from their role of counseling students.

Given this development, it is critical that schools create other open doors for help, such as reorganizing the assignment of counselors so there is a cadre who are designated as individual and group counselors for students and parents, and those who serve as trainers to prepare teachers as advisors and students as peer helpers. Many teens need intervention now and the pathways to sources of help must be easily accessible, welcoming, and trustworthy.

However, the many open doors now needed are not possible given the outdated counseling program model begun in the 1950s that is still very much alive today. This system is based on the theme that all counselors are created equal and have the same level of counseling skills and it is used to assign students to counselors by grade or alphabet, not according to the skills that individual counselors possess.

In this system counselors who are well trained to offer personal counseling become easily transformed into being responsible for assigning students to classes, discipline, college admissions, and so on. These are the activities that counselors soon learn to be successful at in order to keep their jobs as key members of the school's bureaucracy.

Since the inception of the school counseling program in the 1950s, counselors have assumed a leadership role as the point persons in guiding students into the right classes, colleges, or vocations. It became a system that had little time for personal counseling; it became a nuts-and-bolts operation. The nuts and bolts were educational-occupational information and counseling for a realistic future. General education counseling emerged as the main counseling priority in the schools.

As a result new counselors soon learn that they are not really responsible for or expected to offer personal counseling to students. One high school counselor reported:

> It's not really a priority for our counselors. If it happens, fine, but the job is all about increasing the numbers of kids being assigned to classes in which they can succeed, increasing test scores and college admission numbers, and decreasing the number of discipline problems and absentees. I was trained in grad school to provide interventions and group counseling but that's not what my job is all about. I've become a paper pusher. I see my dream of helping kids being buried under a pile of paper.

> The school is only interested in my numbers for what I call the big five: scheduling, college admissions, testing, career choices, and discipline. No one cares about how many kids I see for personal counseling. If I am seen spending

too much time seeing kids for personal counseling and ignoring my big five
duties, I'll be in big trouble. Got to go along with what this job is all about.

As this counselor painfully pointed out, the personal counseling of students
gets relegated to a low priority. In many schools no one in leadership is
asking counselors for the number of students they are seeing for personal
counseling and as a result counselors realize it is not a priority. They keep up
with their big five responsibilities because that's the ticket to tenure and
survival.

Guidance programs have become the vehicle to "sell" the school's big-
five brand to school boards, parents, taxpayers, and even to themselves—that
they are a successful and winning institution. Passing budgets is the driving
force behind the work of today's school counselors.

We don't hear school superintendents speaking at high school graduations
about the number of students receiving personal counseling or intervention.
What we usually hear is how many students were accepted to college, the
scholarships and financial aid received, which students excelled in academics
as well as sports, music, art, and so on. The focus is on students who are high
achievers and bring ongoing positive media attention to themselves and the
school.

One might say that secondary schools ride the successes of these high
achievers as the vehicle to pass school budgets. High achievers demand and
get the guidance services they need to compete for admission to competitive
colleges, win scholarships, and be standard bearers waving the flag of success for the school and community. The guidance programs in many schools
are geared to help the best and brightest. They are the ones providing an
ongoing source of "good news" for the school.

However, this good-news-only approach comes with a high cost that is
often overlooked and can serve to derail the main mission of a caring
school—educating and guiding all students to be all they can be. In this "only
good news" world, troubled teens need to look elsewhere for help. Many are
not newsmakers whose activities and successes support their school's positive profile. They are simply kids looking for a caring, welcoming adult who
can provide them with a trusting, safe place, a respite where they can forge a
new plan for life. Their story is not a good news story filled with many
successes. It is a story they know needs changing and hope for a new beginning, but for many of them, the hope they need has eluded them so far.

The dark side of this good-news process causes once-caring schools and
their staff to abandon their major focus on helping kids and turn their energy
and mission into becoming a sales machine for survival. Selling their school
as a product becomes the number-one priority. Over time school administrators and staff come to believe what their public relations gurus are promot-

ing. They become smitten with these positive reviews rather than staying current in their classrooms.

Often these schools take on an aura that they are number one and will never change. But there is a danger in reading one's positive reviews. One comes to believe naively that only good things will continue to happen in one's work. The same goes for educators.

Administrators and staff come to believe the constant hope, dazzle, and self-promotion and deny the dark reality of their marginal students. They gradually lose focus and interest in those who are not good-news kids and their stories. Their lives are not newsworthy. They are the "bad news" kids, kids who live at the margins of school and community life, who act out; fail courses; cause mischief and trouble; have alcohol, tobacco, and drug addictions; have poor health, eating disorders, obesity, and so on.

They are the disenfranchised kids who have no real constituency in the school. They are labeled as "those kids" who don't participate in good-news program—sports, the arts, community service, and peer mediation. They don't make the honor roll or receive any public accolades. Their names and the names of their parents never appear in the good-news reports. That's only for the "other" kids.

Hubris does its work and gradually sets the tone for the school and staff. There is so much effort and push by the staff to save themselves and their school that the process often has a negative impact on their classroom teaching. Unexpected consequences arrive. Often they take the form of settling, laziness, drifting, and abandoning the marginal kids who need help, care, and energy the most.

Sure, the school's public relations ongoing good-news reporting promotes a school that allows no child to fall through the cracks, but the marginal kids and a few caring administrators and teachers know differently. They know their school operates in two different worlds—one for the good-news kids and one for the no-good-news kids.

This process often alters the helping behaviors of once-caring educators. They pretend they haven't changed, that they love and care for all their kids, but the school they once knew now exists in name only. The good-news process has become an unwanted visitor. It's now all about fame for the best and brightest, and they are sucked into the process, ready or not. Consciously or not, they use the stories of the best and brightest students as the ticket to the survival of the school and themselves.

This barrage of good-news rhetoric results in a school world in which troubled teens seeking help shift to other professionals in the school. It's a quiet drift and exit of troubled students from the guidance office. They stop showing up and the school's grapevine guides them to where they can get the help they need. In the process they learn an important lesson in life: avoid those people and settings that can't help you solve your problems and find those settings and people who can. Stop wasting your time knocking on the wrong door.

As the "Counseling at the Crossroads" report suggests, students quickly learn what doors are open for help. Usually they are caring teachers who believe they are skilled and capable of delivering help and are eager to do so. They don't look the other way when they observe a teen headed for trouble or fall back on the excuse that they are only academic teachers paid to teach subject matter, not to help. They don't use the excuse, "That's the job of the guidance counselor, not mine."

These caring teachers who are willing to help are "angel teachers," described in my book *Angel Teachers: Educators Who Care about Troubled Teens*.[4] They are well known throughout the school grapevine as the "go-to" teachers, and teens in trouble seek them out. They are the "go-to" people as the counseling service becomes more administration-oriented and the distance between teens and the counseling office increases. This results in three very different and separate worlds that pass each other but don't connect:

1. a world in which secondary school, particularly high school, counselors focus their work on promoting the business aspects of the school, such as increasing college admissions and test scores;
2. a world in which troubled teens have abandoned the counseling office and are seeking caring and skilled teachers to show them the way; and
3. a world in which counselors highly trained in personal counseling interventions find themselves trapped in a quasi-administrative role.

In today's complex school world, angel teachers have emerged as a valuable intervention resource to help troubled teens.

As educators we know teenagers face many developmental issues as they navigate their paths to adult life. They sometimes find themselves heading toward the margins of school life due to a myriad of problems: school failure; poor peer relations; academic pressure to succeed; acting-out behaviors; and family problems that can lead to risky behavior in seeking out relief with drugs, alcohol, and tobacco addictions. These solutions may at first quiet their demons but over time they further complicate their young lives and offer little relief, only more pain and increased isolation.

These kinds of problems can visit any member of the school community, not just the so-called at-risk students. They can affect the high-achieving students who are the school's standard bearers; the star athletes; average students who are known as well behaved, good kids who offer no trouble; acting-out students who create mischief; failing students on the road to dropping out; and students addicted to drugs, alcohol, or tobacco. No one is immune to risk and taking a harmful path when the bottom falls out of their lives.

They all need help, support, and guidance from caring and experienced educators to help them redirect their lives before their problems become out of control, unmanageable. Often teachers who have a reputation for helping teens in trouble are very visible in the school hallways, the cafeteria, and extracurricular activities. They know how to deliver help in a quiet, trusting, supportive manner, and they know how to refer teens who may need more help than they can offer.

These angel teachers are a guiding spirit and influence on troubled teens. They know them well, look out for them, and encourage them to come to school and be achievers even when their personal and school lives are in disarray. Sadly though, there aren't enough angel teachers in our schools who are able to intervene to help troubled students; we need more of them.

There are angel teachers to be found in every high school, junior high, and middle school in America. When observing students and student-teacher interactions in these schools, one often hears a student advising a peer, "Go see Mr. Toomey or Ms. Tracy; they know how to help kids with problems. You can trust them. They know the deal, believe me. Let me take you up to Mr. Toomey's room after school. He's my academic advisor. You'll feel better after talking to him."

Students are savvy about who delivers help and who doesn't in their schools. They know the drill. Although the school's public relations information suggests that guidance counselors, social workers, and school psychologists are the designated helpers for students in trouble, students know that counselors have been limited by having too many administrative duties.

Students also understand that budget cuts have reduced the number of counselors and forced social workers and psychologists to serve in many different district buildings during their work week. Help for a potentially suicidal student may be delayed because the psychologist is working in a school building miles away. When students need help they understand that the help they need right now is often not available in the offices of the designated helpers.

Students understand this situation and look to other sources of help, such as angel teachers who operate quietly under the radar. They work like doctors in a field hospital in a war zone. Like soldiers wounded in battle, teens come to angel teachers in droves because they know they can be seen quickly, given an antidote to lessen their pain and fears, and given a prescription for recovery. Even if troubled teens at first decide they don't want further help right now, they know where to go when trouble strikes again.

War zones exist in the lives of many teens. Maybe they are not being shot at with bullets and bombs, although some are, but they are victims of abuse that comes in many forms and can tear apart their hopes, dreams, and once-safe worlds. Sometimes a physical wound in battle hurts less than a barrage of hurtful words or a slap across the face. Wounds in battle can be seen clearly; the blood and pain cannot be masked. But wounds suffered by teens from harsh words or physical abuse are often hidden—except to angel teachers, who know their students well and can see the emotional pain in their eyes and demeanor, their desire to be left alone and isolated in their misery and denial, and their fears of having to return to the scene of the abuse when school ends for the day.

They may be going home to more of the same abuse, being bullied on the school bus, called all kinds of derogatory names, or feeling unable to end a so-called romantic relationship in which they are being forced to enter a sexual relationship and being physically coerced if they refuse. Most teen problems don't get better without help and often they get worse. Teens need adults who know them well and who look out for them, who can pull them aside and say, "Let's talk. You look pretty shook up. How about my room at 2:30? I'm not taking no for an answer. We're in this together. I can see you need help and my guess is that you know it too. Let me help you, okay?"

Angel teachers can help troubled teens get the help they need. They do not try to supplant or take over the role of the designated helpers in the school. They are not after a "super-counselor" role that pretends to be an expert about teen problems. They are simply answering a calling to be of service and doing what is required when they see a teen in trouble.

The reality they and their students face is that in many schools the helping roles of counselors, social workers, and school psychologists have been downgraded. Angel teachers are stepping into a helping vacuum created by an overburdened school bureaucracy.

The counseling role of counselors has taken the biggest hit. Many counselors express bewilderment at being targets of hostility from parents and community members because they are unable to offer more students necessary intervention. They feel they are being wrongly accused of choosing to spend their time on administrative tasks and abandoning their personal counseling role.

Many of these caring professionals feel angry, saddened, and betrayed because they simply can't deliver the kinds of help they were trained to provide. They feel boxed into a no-win situation, asked to accomplish a task but lacking the capacity to do the task successfully.

While this candid assessment of the helping process in the schools has been given little attention, it should come as no surprise. Counselors know it; students know it; teachers know it; administrators know it. In my own work history, I have observed the need for counselors to intervene and offer counseling when large secondary schools, many with over 2,500 students, were being torn apart in the 1960s with student rebellion and the increase in drugs and personal problems.

Since that time the counseling role has dwindled as counselors have been increasingly called upon to manage the bureaucratic aspects of these large schools. Much of the counselor's role today is to serve as an arm of the school's public relations and political efforts to guarantee public support. It's clearly an important role amid today's growing public outcry for budget cuts but it's not a role that includes much if any personal counseling.

However, organizational life being what it is, organizations tend to stay with what they know and use the same sales pitch every year to define the helping process for students, even when the helping process has moved in a different direction. That angel teachers find their niche helping troubled teens demonstrates that people within the organization often change more than the organization itself.

They seek to have a direct impact on matters that touch their professional lives, and they want direct participation and influence. They have the skills to lead, to help, and they are not content to be foot soldiers. As angel teachers they believe that they and many teachers serving on the front lines have the resources and practical know-how to solve many of the problems teens bring to their schools.

Some counselors do prefer a quasi-administrative role instead of offering personal counseling because of their own interests in becoming administrators. But many counselors would welcome the professional freedom to be involved with troubled teens by offering individual and group counseling. Most have been trained in graduate programs emphasizing counseling of students as a priority; they arrive in the school environment and find themselves in a role far different from their training, career aspirations, and personal and professional hopes and dreams.

They became counselors to help kids but find themselves pushing paper and sitting in front of a computer all day. It's ironic that counselors, who were initially identified in the creation of large high schools in the 1950s as having the chief role of counseling students, have gradually lost or given up that role, leaving a vacuum now being filled by angel teachers.

Neither the overwhelmed administrators nor the passive guidance counselors are the primary cause of this problem. Rather, they are victims—as are students, parents, and at-risk educators—of a helping system conceived in the 1950s with the advent of the large high school model. This model has been out of date since the 1970s but persists as the "model of choice" for school guidance and counseling programs, despite its being incapable of delivering the services now needed.

There needs to be a change in the way school guidance and counseling programs are organized so that personal counseling can be restored as a priority service and the quasi-administrative role of student scheduling, college admissions, and mandated testing necessary to keep the school organization running smoothly can be maintained. It can be a dual role in which the role of some counselors is to provide personal counseling, and that of others, who may prefer the quasi-administrative tasks, the scheduling, testing, and so on.

Moving from the 1950s big-five priorities into the new paradigm will not be an easy task for school leaders seeking a more inclusive counseling service for all students. Resistance is sure to come from many counselors, school administrators, parents, community members, and even high-achieving students. This is understandable. The big-five counseling model is what they know. It has been a guidance-program brand name for many years. But it is an out-of-date model that is a lose-lose plan for all:

- administrators searching to increase intervention services for troubled teens;
- counselors eager to put their personal counseling skills to work helping troubled teens;
- troubled teens and parents seeking intervention;
- high-achieving students with personal problems, who need intervention to reduce the pressures of being a standard bearer and having to pretend to be problem-free; and
- skilled teachers who want to be involved as creditable helpers in the school intervention team.

Researchers Zuboff and Maxmin[5] provide some helpful observations on how organizations can forge a new model to supersede antiquated institutional barriers and self-protective mentalities. Clearly they apply to the current model used by school districts:

- "Organizations are like all living systems. . . . Every living system has its own unique 'deep structure,' a high durable order that expresses its internal organization as well as the basic activities that define its existence and governs its interactions with the environment."
- "Occasionally . . . the system experiences a wholesale transformation of its deep structure, which must be disassembled in order for any fundamental changes to be accomplished."
- "Like other living systems . . . it is organized to reproduce itself at all costs, even when it is commercially irrational to do so. It is through these processes . . . that organizations defy change, even when they say they are changing."
- "Typically people in organizations do not see what's coming. Events are not read as an indication that people should change what they are doing or how they are thinking. On the contrary, challenging events are often regarded as a signal that people should do more of the same thing they already know how to do, only do it more assiduously than before. Sometimes these responses to grave challenges are deeply unhealthy and actual-

ly weaken the person, group or system, but people feel compelled to reproduce what they already know."

- "At the dawn of the twenty-first century, people have new dreams. . . . Today's people experience themselves first as individuals and long for 'psychological determination.' . . . As a result of these new dreams a chasm has opened up between people and the organizations upon which they depend. People have undergone a discontinuity in mentality but organizations have not. . . . Individuals reach out from the intricacy of their lives in search of understanding, accommodation, and support, but the complexity of their needs and desire is ignored."
- People have changed more than the organizations upon which their well-being depends. Today's individuals "reject organizational mediation, seeking instead to have a direct impact upon matters that touch [their lives]. They demand a high quality of direct participation and influence. They have the skills to lead, confer and discuss, and they are not content to be foot soldiers."
- They believe in leadership that is "bottom-up" rather than "top-down," preferring collective participation of average people to solve the problems.

The picture offered in these comments by Zuboff and Maxmin seems to describe the organization problem in our schools. Their remedy deserves consideration by school boards, administrators, teacher-union leaders, and teacher leaders. They suggest that "old organizations have become sufficiently insulated and self-congratulatory to ignore the chasm that has formed between their practices, invented by mass society, and the new people it has spawned. . . . The new individuals are being blamed for the problems of the old organization when the facts suggest the opposite."

Yet, as Zuboff and Maxmin say, "Letting go of the past is painful. . . . People know how to operate in the system that already exists. They know how to compete and how to succeed in that system. Changing the deep structure of a system is threatening to everyone. There will be new winners and losers, new skills to learn, new ranking rules. These fears are compounded by the fact that many people have invested their entire careers in the old structures. . . . Change belittles their lifetime achievement. It diminishes all that they have sacrificed."

Zuboff and Maxmin also say that another reason people avoid deep structure change "involves the relationships and commitments that people have developed both inside and outside the system. Individuals frequently find it difficult to change because they are afraid of disappointing the people closes to them, such as marital partners or professional colleagues. If a person has been valued by important others, he tends to fear the loss of that positive regard if he undergoes change and possibly develops new directions."

The current guidance-program model must be disassembled in order for fundamental change to be accomplished. Like all other systems, guidance systems are organized to reproduce themselves at all costs, even when it is irrational to do so. Guidance organizations will defy change, even when they say they are changing. As Zuboff and Maxmin suggest, the advent of a change process is often regarded as a signal that counselors should do the same thing they already know how to do.

Many counselors will feel compelled to reproduce what they already know after eyeing my plan and paradigm for change. There is both institutional and professional pressure on them to stay their present course. There is tremendous pressure from colleges and universities to keep counselors in the role of quasi-administrators and college-admission experts and relegate personal counseling to a minor or even nonexistent role, a "nice if we could offer kids more personal counseling but who has time" role.

The reality is that many members of the higher-education community see guidance counselors as their ticket to maintaining their student enrollment and are increasing their wooing approach. Intentionally or not, college-admissions directors want guidance counselors focused on guiding students into their colleges, not spending time solving personal problems. And they continuously work at shoring up this image of the counselor's role with perks.

Gregg Winter describes the wooing process used by college admissions directors such as Victor I. Davolt of Regis University, located in Denver, Colorado.[6] Winter reports that for the past two years Davolt has been playing host to school guidance counselors, the "extremely influential" people he hopes will send more students to his ninety-acre campus. He flies them in from around the country to meet the faculty and review the curriculum.

But he also includes skiing on the world-famous slopes of Vail, snowmobiling and spending time at a spa, and getting a facial or massage, all courtesy of the university. Davolt also treats counselors to professional hockey games and rooms at luxury hotels.

Winter observes that although the image of the admissions process is often one of high school counselors sidling up to colleges in hopes of gaining an advantage for their students, the reality is sometimes the other way around. Colleges are so intent on getting not just enough applicants, but the best ones, that some are lavishing perks on guidance counselors.

For example, when the admissions staff at Center City College in Danville, Kentucky, invites guidance counselors to visit, it puts them up in a bed and breakfast and takes them golfing at a country club and to a racetrack. It even gives them a small stake, around fifty dollars, so they can gamble on the horses. Goucher College in Towson, Maryland, takes visiting counselors to the theater, the symphony, and Baltimore Orioles games, and rents out the Rock and Roll Hall of Fame and museum for a night to thank counselors.

Ralph S. Figueroa, director of college guidance at Albuquerque Academy, a private school in New Mexico, suggests, "We can't help but be swayed by the people who are nice to us, who buy nice things for us."

These college excursions offer short-term but tangible rewards for guidance counselors in that they provide an open door through which they can escape from their often-hectic school life and instead can be wined and dined and made to feel they are needed and appreciated. Principals and counselor reformers need to be mindful of these powerful pressures when they begin asking counselors to redefine their services.

Many counselors will say that what is needed is the hiring of more counselors to meet the growing personal needs of students. As education reporter Shelly Reese[7] suggests, many counselors don't want new methods; they want more assistance. The problem with this kind of response is that it is based on the notion of expanding resources in a time of increasingly limited resources for schools rather than on an examination of how to use the existing counseling resources to meet current needs.

This response also overlooks the notion that hiring more counselors usually results in more resources being poured into the scheduling and testing aspect of counselors' work, not a shift to more individual and group counseling and intervention. In school reform the quasi-administrator role of the counselor is difficult, if not impossible, to change simply by adding new personnel to do more of the same.

Changing a system is threatening to everyone. There will be new skills to learn and new ways to adapt. Fear and uncertainty are part of the change process. We need to keep in mind that many counselors have invested their entire careers in the old structures. Change belittles their lifetime achievements; it diminishes all they have sacrificed.

As Zuboff and Maxmin remind us, counselors may find it difficult to change because they are afraid of disappointing colleagues close to them. If a counselor has been valued by a colleague, he or she fears the loss of that positive regard if he or she undergoes change and possibly develops in new directions.

Moving from the 1950s guidance and counseling model into a new era will not be easy. A new model needs to be sold to counselors, administrators, and counselor educators. This sales campaign involves presenting a new model that has something in it for them and getting them on board the change process one by one.

This model needs to emphasize how a new role for personal counselors can provide necessary intervention to help students, parents, staff, and even administrators who find themselves caught up in problematic situations that are leading to failure. Skilled guidance counselors who are freed to deliver personal counseling are much needed in today's schools. The cries of troubled members of the school community must be met if we are to improve the achievement of all our students.

Bill Gates, founder of Microsoft, offers the following advice on the need for such an overhaul.

> America's high schools are obsolete. They were designed fifty years ago to meet the needs of another age. Until we design them to meet the needs of the 21st century, we will keep limiting, even ruining, the lives of millions of Americans every year . . . but these are "our" high schools that keep letting kids drop through the cracks and we act as if it can't be helped. We designed these schools, we can redesign them. The basic building of better schools includes making sure kids have a number of adults who know them, who look out for them, and push them to achieve.[8]

However, the path ahead to organizational redesigns to provide more personal counseling to help students will not be an easy road. The 2012 National Survey of School Counselors reports that counselors are often overwhelmed with important but misallocated work, and they are held accountable for the wrong things. In short, although counselors are poised to meaningfully contribute, they are operating with a broken compass. Even if counselors are taking steps to improve efficacy, they feel ill-equipped to quantify and communicate their responsibilities and successes. Hopefully this book provides the needed compass.[9]

NOTES

1. The College Board, "Counseling at the Crossroads," National Office of School Counseling Advocacy, 2011, 6–11, 20, 42.

2. Jean Johnson and Jon Rochkind, "Can I Get a Little Advice Here?," Public Agenda, March 2010, pp. 1–12, available online at www.publicagenda.org/files/can-i-get-a-little-advice-here.pdf (accessed March 21, 2013).

3. Winnie Hu, "Bullying Law Puts New Jersey Schools on Spot," *New York Times*, August 31 2011, pp. 1, 23A, available online at http://www.nytimes.com/2011/08/31/nyregion/bullying-law-puts-new-jersey-schools-on-spot.html?pagewanted=all&_r=0 (accessed March 21, 2013).

4. William L. Fibkins, *Angel Teachers: Educators Who Care About Troubled Teens* (Lanham, MD: Rowman & Littlefield, 2012), 2–6.

5. Shoshana Zuboff and James Maxmin, *The Support Economy: Why Corporations Are Failing Individuals and the Next Episode of Capitalism* (New York: Viking, 2002), 34–36.

6. Gregg Winter, "Wooing of Guidance Counselors Is Raising Profiles and Eyebrows," *New York Times*, July 8, 2004, pp. 1, 18A, available online at www.nytimes.com/2004/07/08/education/08perks.html (accessed March 21, 2013).

7. Shelley Reese, "The Counselors Conundrum: Provide Triage or Full Service Programs," *Middle Ground*, October 1998, pp. 17–19, 24.

8. Bill Gates and Melinda Gates, speech given at the National Education Summit on High Schools, February 26, 2005, available online at www.gatesfoundation.org/media-center/speeches/2005/02/bill-gates-2005-national-education-summit (accessed March 21, 2013).

9. Texas School Counselor Association, "True North: Charting the Course to College and Career Readiness," National Office of School Counseling Advocacy, February 11, 2013, pp.

4–5, available online at www.txca.org/images/Conference/SCC/13/handouts/Martin.pdf (accessed March 21, 2013).

Chapter Two

Personal Counseling for Troubled Students Never Gained a Foothold in School Guidance Programs

Personal counseling for troubled students never gained a foothold in many school guidance and counseling programs that developed in the 1950s and 1960s in our large high schools. While it was given much attention in school media announcements, in reality the quasi-administrative duties of school counselors took top priority. Personal counseling, when it was offered, was intermittent and provided by a few well-trained counselors who saw it as their personal mission. Even then intervention was never given a high priority. It was a limited effort at best, based on the counselor's own determination not to allow needy and troubled students to end up on the margins of school life.

While counselors were being anointed as the experts on students' academic, social, and personal development, the personal and social development parts often took a back seat. An unintended consequence of guidance counselors being seen as the experts on academic, personal, and social development was that caring teachers who had once enjoyed a prominent role in helping students with personal issues were told to stick to teaching their academic subjects and leave the counseling to the experts.

As a result troubled students who attended the large high schools during those years found few open doors for help. Teachers withdrew and did what they were told: stop helping kids; the experts will take care of the counseling domain. Meanwhile, the experts expected to help counsel troubled teens were engulfed by the organizational demands of these new schools.

When students went to the guidance office for help with personal problems, there was little help available. Most students were assigned to counselors by grade or alphabet. If they were lucky, they were assigned to a counselor with the interest and personal counseling skills to help them. If not, these students were forced to look elsewhere, but where?

Not only were the students left on their own, but also so were the counselors who were advocating for an increased personal counseling role in their guidance programs. Both groups were on the fringe, students asking for help and well-trained counselors asking for time and the go-ahead to help them. The new guidance programs promised counseling for all students. However, the dominant role of counselors included activities such as scheduling, college-admission preparation, testing, and career and discipline counseling.

These large schools made it easy for both students and staff to remain anonymous, with little personal connection. It was easy for troubled students and staff to be overlooked amidst the din of selling how good the school was doing.

As the author I suggest in *An Educator's Guide to Understanding the Personal Side of Students' Lives*,[1] the evolution of guidance counseling programs gave little attention to troubled students. The book provides an overview of the ideas, reports, and research by James B. Conant; Robert Hampel; James E. Allen; Arthur G. Powell, Eleanor Farrar, and David K. Cohen; David R. Cook; Harold L. Munson; Harold C. McCully; Diane Ravitch; Gerald Grant; and the American School Counselors Association on how this new counseling movement evolved into a quasi-administrative arm of the school administration with a focus on selecting and sorting students for academic classes, careers, and college acceptance. Personal counseling never achieved a significant role in this new guidance organization. Here's the story:

The emergence of Conant's large comprehensive high school model occurred in the late 1950s. In late October 1957 the Soviets launched Sputnik, the first space satellite. Sputnik became an instant metaphor for the poor quality of America's schools. Overnight a clamor arose for higher academic standards and greater attention to mathematics, science, and foreign language in schools.

In response to these criticisms, James B. Conant, former president of Harvard, wrote in his book *The American High School Today*[2] that no basic changes were necessary. He suggested instead that small high schools should be eliminated and that no high school should have a graduating class of fewer than one hundred students. This would have resulted in reducing the number of high schools in the United States by more than half. His proposed comprehensive high schools would offer a strong academic program for the academically gifted students and a variety of general and technical courses for the majority who were not.

Conant also suggested that every high school have a good counseling program to ensure that students were guided into the right programs. He recommended that there should be one full-time counselor for every 250 to 300 students in the high school. They should be familiar with the use of tests and measurements to assess the aptitudes and achievement of pupils. In his vision, all students would take a basic required course of four years of English, three or four years of social studies, one year of science, and one year of math. Everything else would be an elective and it would be up to the guidance staff, using their tests, to make sure the students chose the appropriate electives.

Conant felt that only 15 percent of high school students had the mental ability to take rigorous courses in math, science, and foreign languages. Perhaps another 10 to 20 percent might stretch to take an academic program as well. But the 65 to 75 percent of students should take courses in marketable skills. He warned that ambitious parents might attempt to get their children enrolled in advanced mathematics, physics, and foreign languages but that school officials must resist their entreaties.

Counselors would have to be prepared to persuade overly ambitious parents that their children were not academically talented. Conant, speaking primarily about suburban high schools, suggested that one of the main tasks of the guidance counselors was college placement. In order to keep lines of communication open with these institutions and to follow high school graduates to college, the services of one person working full time on college placement were required.

Conant's proposals put strong pressure on state and local officials to get rid of small high schools because they could not provide a full array of academic, vocational, and general courses. His report was welcomed by educators because its message was reassuring. Any changes needed were minor and would conform to the basic philosophical premise that had ruled American education for more than a generation.

Conant followed up his recommendations in 1967 with his book *The Comprehensive High School: A Second Report to Interested Citizens.*[3] He reported that his research found that his recommendation of one full-time counselor for every 250 to 300 students was not being followed. In his sample of 2,000 schools, in only 3.4 percent of them was the ratio 1 to 299 or less.

The changes proposed by Conant were not minor. The creation of large schools had unintended consequences for both students and teachers. In small high schools students were know by many adults in the school; they were not anonymous. In the large comprehensive high schools the intimate environment of the small school was lost. Students were often bused long distances and interacted with students from different communities, backgrounds, cultures, and values.

The same was true for teachers. In the small schools they interacted on a personal and intimate basis with their students; they often lived in the community and served as role models while acting as coaches and club leaders. In the large high schools they also lost the feeling of closeness and community; closeness with students became more difficult.

As a result subject-matter-teaching defined their role. They no longer provided intimate, supportive, and helpful interactions with students. That became the role of the counselors, at least in theory. The primary role of counselors, however, was to guide students into the right programs. Personal counseling was, of necessity, given less attention. Priority was given to college placement and only the most troubled students in crisis saw the counselor for personal counseling.

The large comprehensive high schools certainly brought with them new facilities and expanded curriculum offerings. But they brought with them isolation of students and teachers from one another. Teachers had fewer opportunities to observe and identify students who were experiencing personal and well-being problems that affected their academic performance. Students experienced fewer opportunities to develop close, trusting relationships with teachers who cared about them. And counselors found themselves unable to provide the personal counseling necessary while also fulfilling their obligation to route students into appropriate placements.

Students who had personal problems that affected their academic performance were too often routed into nonacademic programs or encouraged to drop out. The helping and advising skills of teachers were underutilized. They were told, often in no uncertain terms, to stick to teaching and leave counseling to the counselors. It turned into a no-win situation for all—students, teachers, and counselors.

Education historian Robert Hampel pointed out that guidance counselors became a powerful force in the schools despite the fact that Conant's recommendation concerning the ration of counselors to students fell short. Numbers of counselors rose faster than the student population in the 1950s and early 1960s. According to Hampel, in 1951–1952 only 17.2 percent of high schools had at least one person devoted half time or more to counseling; by 1966, 65 percent of high schools had counselors.

These changes involved replacing teacher-counselors with full-time counselors. In the 1930s and 1940s many teachers acted as counselors for one or two periods as part of their teaching assignment and administrators often took on counseling roles as well. By the 1960s guidance was mainly the province of full-time specialists. Another result was the proliferation of journals, associations, training programs, and certification laws addressed to the counseling profession.

Hampel also points out that these newly created counseling departments did not dispense survival skills or address the emotional problems of teens, as had been envisioned by reformers. By 1957, with the launch of Sputnik, counselors spent most of their time advising students on course selection and college placement. They were closely aligned with the school administration.

Their new position of power was described by Dr. James E. Allen, commissioner of education of the New York State Department of Education, this way: Guidance is looked upon by the laymen, as well as those in education, as an integral and vital part of the educational process. The education profession and the public have come to expect substantial contributions from guidance in assisting boys and girls toward optimum development for their own fulfillment and for their economic and social contributions.

In contrast, the 1964 American School Counselor Association's Statement of Policy for Secondary School Counselors describes counselors as being concerned with and accepting responsibility for all students and their developmental needs and problems. The policy cites the counselor's responsibility for becoming involved with all students and their behaviors.

In reality counselors rarely analyzed teenagers' emotions to the extent envisioned by reformers or recommended by their professional associations. The counselor's role in the new comprehensive high schools was, as mentioned earlier, quasi-administrative with a focus on testing, scheduling, and college placement.

Arthur G. Powell, Eleanor Farrar, and David K. Cohen also suggest that in today's high schools, the advising portion of counselor responsibilities mostly consists of the logistics of scheduling and meeting graduation requirements. Students complain that their counselors know nothing about them, seeing them at the beginning of the year and not again. One girl thought of her counselor as a kind of traffic cop telling her when to go and when to stop, which roads were open and which were blocked. "If I had a problem he'd be the last one I'd go to," she said. The reason she gave was, "He doesn't know me. He wouldn't be able to help."

Part of the problem, as Powell, Farrar, and Cohen point out, is sheer numbers. At one school the student-to-counselor ration was 420 to 1. the objective of many counseling departments is to see each student once a year in a conference that typically, as one counselor suggests, takes ten minutes. In addition to sheer numbers, counselors complain with equal vehemence about the paperwork loaded upon them. One estimated that fully 75 percent of her time was spent keeping records, and others pointed to the significant scheduling and monitoring activities required by the special-needs legislation.

Yet, despite these odds, some of the nearly eight thousand counselors trained at university counselor education institutes sponsored by the National Defense Education Act in the 1960s did try to change their quasi-administrator role. As counselor educator David R. Cook states, they were called change agents who could serve as creative critics, feedback agents, ombudsmen/student advocates, and managers of conflict in addition to their regular guidance duties.

Their work was to help the school organization understand and respond to increasing racial conflicts and student unrest. They tried to implement new counseling approaches—such as group counseling and sensitivity training for teachers, group counseling for students, and training students as peer helpers—into their guidance programs.

However, these bold and risky efforts by a small cadre of counselors to add a more personal connection between teachers and students was doomed to failure because of the pressing organizational demands identified by Powell, Farrar, and Cohen. Yes, counselor educators such as Cook could suggest that the guidance counselor who presumes that he can fulfill his role in the school by remaining in his office and seeing students one at a time is already an anachronism. When some counselors did move out of their offices and begin to offer group counseling to teachers and students, they encountered great resistance from colleagues who were more comfortable with their sorting-and-selecting side.

They often found themselves without cover and political support from directors of guidance and school administrators who wanted these counselors back in their offices, dealing with the nuts and bolts of the guidance operation, not offering counseling to teachers and students that might bring calls for changes in the existing and increasingly vulnerable school climate. I believe it is safe to say that these pioneer counselors were out of step with the selecting-and-sorting counseling model that took hold in the 1960s and still exists today.

Counselor educator Harold L. Munson describes the lost opportunities to utilize the helping and advising role of teachers with the emergence of counselors as the primary source of help for students. He suggests that teachers do have very specific classroom opportunities to become engaged with individual students in ways that not only facilitate the learning process of individual students but also can be personally relevant and enhancing to him or her. He also suggests that teachers who care about a student or students who care about a teacher (or feel that a teacher cares about them) are more apt to communicate about very meaningful and sometimes confidential topics. They may develop very significant relationships. Such communication should be encouraged.

Teachers are human. They can be accepting, understanding, and trusting. Some teachers, if we can accept the reports of youth, are better at providing these conditions than some school counselors. If a teacher can relate to a student in this manner, he or she should be free to do so. To restrict such relationships is to infringe on the freedom of the teacher and destroy the humanness of the teaching/learning process. Perhaps his or her communication skills and techniques are not professionally developed, yet he or she has the potentiality for a human relationship with every student.

Communication about the student's progress, ability, and interest in the subject may spill over to personal matters outside the usual realm of teacher concern and responsibility. This should be anticipated and when the teacher feels capable and confident to deal with these issues, he or she should be encouraged to do so. This is counseling, even though it may be limited to the topics relevant to the individual's learning experience.

Munson cautions, however, that this role is rapidly being taken away from teachers. He suggests that while many students are seeking to communicate with teachers, with increasing frequency teachers are urged to refer students with learning irregularities, with unsatisfactory achievement, and with a host of other concerns to the school counselor. As Munson wisely suggests, the danger here lies in absolving the teacher of his or her rightful and expected guidance responsibilities.

The message, while not always overt or openly expressed, has become rather clear. Even when this is calculated only for students with problems that extend beyond the proficiency of the teachers, the expectations that students are "treated" in the guidance office leaves the developmental needs of youth too often unattended in the classroom. And it raises considerable doubt, fear, and guilt in the minds of teachers who respond or feel they must respond to students.

Teachers have been warned repeatedly that they are not counselors and thus, with the advent of guidance, they have become increasingly wary and cautious. Counseling has increasingly been a territorial claim of the school counselor, accordingly reducing the involvement of many teachers in any communication with their students that could be interpreted as counseling.

As the guidance movement has developed, and particularly as the counseling function has become a more important and significant element in the total guidance activity, arguments against teacher involvement in student counseling have been cited. It is almost as if teachers have been warned against any kind of human involvement wherein they can communicate with their students about goals, interests, abilities, values, feelings, and behaviors. It is no wonder that they have become less sure of their own human relationships with their students. It is no wonder they have become cautious and concerned.

Munson's cogent observations about the negating of teachers' helping and advising roles are on target. Munson's comments, made in 1971, could accurately describe the flawed helping relationships that exist in today's secondary schools. Yet I believe that counselors didn't intentionally set out to develop the flawed helping and advising system that remains alive and well in today's secondary schools.

As the American School Counselors Association's policy statement suggests, the original goal of counseling in the secondary schools was to assist all students with their developmental needs and problems. But other powerful forces were at play that forced counselors into a quasi-administrative role. The needs of the nation in the post–World War II and post-Sputnik eras demanded that the schools guide students into the right courses, colleges, and vocations. Students were seen as resources to keep our nation strong militarily and economically. Counselors became the point persons in carrying out the schools' new mandate.

As Cook suggests, counselors emerged as one of the main functionaries in implementing the sorting and allocation of functions in the school. They were caught up in a system that left little time for personal counseling. Counselor educator Harold C. McCully says guidance became a nuts-and-bolts operation. The nuts and bolts were the individual inventory, educational, and occupational information; counseling for a realistic future; matching of individual traits with occupational opportunities; and placement and follow-up.

Cook says general education counseling emerged as the main counseling concern in the schools. As he wisely observed, many counselors who might be adequate to the task of therapeutic counseling found that the demands of the school's situation made it difficult, if not impossible, to carry out this kind of counseling. Cook backs up his assertions with data from the New England Assessment Project:

1. When students were asked, "Has your school counselor helped you find better ways to solve problems about school and other things you've had to face?," 68 percent of students said no and 32 percent said yes.
2. "Did you get help in understanding yourself from your school counselor?" Sixty-one percent said no; 31 percent said yes.
3. "Do you know yourself better as a student as a result of visiting your school counselor?" Sixty-four percent said no; 36 percent said yes.
4. "Can you talk about your real feeling about things with your school counselor?" Forty-three percent said yes; 57 percent said no.

Cook suggests that for the past several years, counselors have been wrapped in an identity crisis, struggling with the question, "What is our role?" He suggests that the professionalization of school counseling has become something of a box in which the school counselor is trapped. The counselor has been seduced into functioning on behalf of the bureaucratic structure of the school. Despite a mountain of rhetoric about meeting the needs of pupils, the reality is that it was the increasing bureaucratization of our school systems that created the demands for guidance services.

Cook, writing in 1971, accurately described conditions for many fine counselors in 2012. The same conditions exist forty-plus years later. As he suggested then, many counselors who might be adequate to the task of therapeutic counseling find that the demands of the school situation make it difficult, if not impossible, to carry out this kind of counseling. And as it exists today, despite a mountain of rhetoric about meeting the needs of pupils, the reality is that it was the increasing bureaucratization of our school system that is still creating the demands for guidance services.

The social, cultural, and political eruptions in the beginning of the 1960s acted to further isolate students from personal and intimate connections with counselors. As Ravitch suggests, the 1960s began with no hint of troubles ahead for schools and society. Educators enjoyed a keen sense of success. They had come closer to providing universal access to high school education than in any generation before them. In 1900 it was a rare youngster, only six out of every one hundred, who earned a high school diploma.

By 1960 an astounding 70 percent of high school students received a high school diploma. For years the system had worked as planned, sending appropriate proportions of students to colleges, farms, factories, shops, domestic service, and homemaking.

But that keen feeling of success and pride fell apart in many high schools in the 1960s. The upheaval of the 1960s changed the public schools in important ways. Confronted with violence, disciplinary problems, and litigation, school officials backed away from acting in locus parentis. In an effort to reduce conflict, academic demands were minimized; students were increasingly left to fend for themselves, without adult guidance.

Observations by Gerald Grant of this turbulent era end this quote. Grant describes the chaos and lack of control at Hamilton High School, the placid and coherent school community of the 1950s that was destroyed by the turbulence of the 1960s. In 1960 Hamilton High was regarded as the leading school in the area. The school was orderly, hallways glistened, and lateness to class was a rarity. Students showed deference to teachers and seldom needed more than a stern glance to correct behavior.

But, after taking steps to increase racial integration, the school was convulsed with riots and violence from 1968 to 1971. Discipline dissolved, respect for teachers evaporated, racial separation increased, many white middle-class students left the school, and administrators had to devote most of their time to disciplining unruly students. In a school that once prided itself on its keen sense of community, adult authority collapsed. As Grant suggests, fearful of litigation, the adults at Hamilton High retreated to their classrooms and closed their doors. The school added new specialists to the staff for counseling and various social activities.

However, adding new specialists for counseling created a new layer of counselors, many part-timers from community mental health agencies who were not a known part of the school community, or full-time educators on a tenure track who lacked supervision by school administrators. They became a cadre working on their own and not integrated into the school community. One director of guidance referred to them as "outside hired guns."

Outsiders were now becoming the key players in offering counseling to the increasing numbers of troubled students. Meanwhile the guidance counselors stuck to their quasi-administrative role, further isolating themselves from troubled students and from the newly arrived counselors who floated through the increasingly hostile and disruptive school environment like apostles out to rescue acting-out students and bring calm and order to the school community. This was not a wise prescription for intervention but rather, in some cases, a rogue, unsupervised group operation with no restrictions on where, when, and what they did to offer students counseling.

The 1960s and 1970s were tough times for schools, educators, students, and parents. The intervention system developed by school guidance and counseling programs was painfully exposed as being not up to the task of intervening to help troubled and acting-out students.

The rising criticism of their failure was only to become more intense with the publication of *A Nation at Risk: The Imperative for Educational Reform*,[4] the 1983 report of President Ronald Reagan's National Commission on Excellence in Education, calling for higher standards and an increased academic emphasis for students. The report revealed a profound crisis in public education, with the problems of high schools receiving the lion's share of attention.

The commission decried the cafeteria-style curriculum in which students could get a large proportion of their credits for graduation through courses such as physical and health education, work experience outside of school, remedial courses, and personal service and development courses such as training for adulthood, bachelor living, marriage, and parenting. High school guidance counselors in particular came in for criticism for not directing more-capable students in rigorous academic classes and leaving them to take an easy path to graduation.

These growing demands for an increase in students' academic achievement continued into the early 2000s with the passage of the No Child Left Behind Act of 2003, which called for accountable high-stake expectations in which every professional in every school would be expected to contribute to the overall strategy for improving school achievement. As a result counselors found themselves once again aligned in improving student achievement.

If the school was unable to deliver an increase in student achievement and test scores, reduce discipline problems, improve student grades and attendance, lower suspension and drop-out rates, reduce failures, and increase college-admission rates, counselors were often at the center of the blame games.

Guidance and counseling programs found themselves in a no-win situation during the late twentieth and early twenty-first centuries, criticized for not being able to intervene and help acting-out students in the 1960s and 1970s and not pushing more-able students into rigorous academic classes in the 1980s and later.

Counselors have taken an unfair beating because of the way their programs were conceived in the 1950s, leaving many counselors unskilled and unprepared for personal counseling and intervention and, in the 1980s, not being aggressive enough as academic counselors for students. What was lacking from the beginning was a counseling paradigm that could respond to the need for both personal counseling for troubled students and guiding them into the right classes, colleges, vocations, etc.

It was a system built for failure as the world and America changed in very dramatic and disturbing ways from the post–World War II era with its conservative values and small-town view of society. The schools were not prepared for such a drastic change in student values, social mores, and lifestyles. Maybe there was nothing more the schools could have done, given the way they were organized.

Moving on is now required. Guidance counselors were not responsible for the organizational failures of the past. They were like children born into a dysfunctional family and asked to solve its problems without the skills and resources needed. And personal counseling was the orphan in this dysfunctional family, never really connected or valued.

However, moving on first requires counselors to learn from past experience. As Zuboff and Maxmin remind us in chapter 1, systems are organized to reproduce themselves at all costs, even when it is commercially irrational to do so. Organizations defy change even when they say they are changing. Counselor leaders need to remember that the large comprehensive school guidance and counseling model developed under Conant's leadership did not prove to be a successful model for a changing country. But amazingly, it is still the model of choice in 2013.

Today's guidance and counseling programs need a new model if they are to be a viable service for students, parents, teachers, and administrators. One of the major goals should be for counselors to reexamine their current roles and functions and assess what works and what doesn't, not to keep doing what is not working.

As researcher Susan C. Whiston[5] suggests, counselors continue to do everything. Most counselors report that their days go by with a whirlwind of activities. They wonder at the end of the day what they have accomplished. One of the reasons for this is the multiple expectations that people have of school counselors. And most counselors have a basic desire to help.

Whiston states that one of the strengths of school counselors is their dedication and willingness to pitch in and help. This strength is also a weakness, for many counselors try to manage multiple responsibilities and over-whelming caseloads as best they can. This make-do attitude often results in some responsibilities being neglected because of conflicting expectations and complex duties.

Whiston suggests a remedy to this problem by saying it may be an appropriate time to better educate administrators, policymakers, parents, and other stakeholders about the plight of school counselors. She says it might be interesting to see a school board's reaction to statements such as, "Although school counselors are responsible for academic, career, and personal/social development, our rations are too high in the district to provide all three, so the board needs to decide which of these three areas students do not need." A school counselor might say to a principal, "It is impossible to meet the needs of all children, so can you please select the students who do not need assistance?"

Whiston advises that it would be unwise to use either of these statements. But counselors should consider what they can do to have others understand the problems and unrealistic expectations and the negative effects of adding nonguidance activities to a counselor's responsibilities.

Whiston closes by suggesting that there may be further development of federal and state children and family legislation that could lead to a dramatic expansion of psychological services in schools. An important concern is whether school counselors would be involved in these activities or relegated to a noncounseling duty. Whiston says she is not suggesting that academic and career development should be abandoned in order to provide only personal/social interventions. On the other hand, she says she does not believe personal/social development should be underemphasized in order to respond to pressure to increase test scores.

What Whiston misses in her report is that the guidance and counseling system is a fail-fail system not only for committed, caring counselors but also for their students, parents, colleagues, and administrators. In trying to do everything, something has to give, and what is lost is the personal/social development of students. School boards and principals are facing increasing demands to improve academic achievement and test scores, and they expect counselors to lead this charge. Going to school board meetings and to building principals to ask for lower caseloads and diminished responsibilities in this day of tight budgets is a fruitless task.

In these tough times the only way out is for counselors to fix their present system so it works. They have to help themselves. Administrators and school board members have too much on their plates and they are not going to listen to requests to make counselors' jobs easier as their own jobs get increasingly more difficult and politicized.

The bottom line is that counselors can't continue to do everything and be successful in the present system. As Whiston suggests, if they can't develop a system that includes personal/social intervention, that will be relegated to noncounseling duties in the school's organizational chart. Unfortunately, Whiston is a victim of the present system as well by implying that academic and career development not be abandoned and personal/social intervention not be underemphasized in order to respond to pressure to increase test scores. This is a prayer that doesn't have a chance of being answered without major changes in the way counselors organize their work.

When systems and people in these systems try to do everything, something has to give. Although Whiston wants academic and personal/social intervention to succeed on an equal basis, that's not going to happen in the present system no matter how hard counselors try. As Whiston writes, "This make-do attitude often results in some responsibilities being neglected." These responsibilities are not being neglected, as she states, because of "conflicting expectations and complex duties." I believe they are being neglected because the system is rigged to answer the academic needs of students, not their social, physical, and emotional well-being, even though these developmental needs have a huge impact on achievement.

Counselors are bright, savvy people. They know this. They have to find what works and be sold on a new path that can make them players again before they are relegated to a guidance and counseling role minus the counseling.

Whiston also suggests that we need more research in order to verify how counselors are spending their time. She says that once more is known about which activities are supported, practitioners can argue more persuasively against being saddled with activities that do not facilitate human development. That's a nice idea but in the tough politics of today's school world, counselors are being given a list of activities that can help their schools to be safe and caring, raise achievement, and intervene to help students with personal/social development. It's up to them to find the right system to make these activities work.

The reality is that they are saddled with these tasks. They have to figure it out or in the long run they will disappear as the intervention specialists they are claimed to be.

The following are some quotes from counselors in the field that speak to the issue of being unable to offer personal counseling to troubled students due to too much paperwork and noncounseling demands. The comments appeared on Linkedin.com[6] in response to a question from a counselor, "Do you have to do so many things other than counseling that you never have time to be a counselor?"

The counselor described her own role:

> My job roles include all students in our district, which has about 550 students
> in Pre-K through 12; response to intervention 5th through 12th; 504 for the

district; GT for the district; and I'm the district testing coordinator. I also serve on three district committees and the Education Foundation. Oh, and I have afternoon hallway duty at one school a few times a year. Is that totally atypical, or are there some of you that wear lots of hats, too? My primary office is at the high school, so I also act as registrar and change schedules.

Here are some of the responses to her query.

Hi. It's as you are experiencing, a no-win situation for you and other counselors. The problem is our guidance and counseling programs are organized on a 1950 model and out of date, incapable of meeting the needs of today's troubled students, parents, and educators. Counselors like you are the present day victims of this system and no matter how hard you may try to meet the personal and well-being needs of teens, paperwork and quasi-administrative duties always win out. Result? Personal counseling has become a low priority as counseling programs have increasingly become a "paper work" arm of the administrations.

I feel like I have great teachers who pick up a lot of my slack with the students in their classes as far as individual counseling goes. Plus, each campus principal is pretty good with reasoning with them. That's how I live with not being able to spend the time I need to actually counsel.

I often think that if there is a job that no administrator want to do, they stick it on the counselor.

I have had principals laugh when I shared a value that counselors should only wear one hat. . . . The perception needs to be changed by us. We need to make our program important. Survey teachers—ask what they need from the counseling center. Someone said to me once, "Look and sounds like you are not doing your job the way you want to." Couldn't have said it better. Value what you were trained for and promote that. Sounds easy . . . yea! We as counselors need to support each other and I'm with Laura. Let's brainstorm and promote counseling.

I sympathize. Being in the HS setting myself, it is a constant battle to balance the counseling aspect with other responsibilities of the job. I have come to realize that much of the job is broken down into counseling at school, administrative work outside of the school day. And scheduling—eeesh, that is an animal of its own. It's tough but hang in there. The interaction with the older kids—watching them mature and come into their own—is amazing.

I am itinerant this year. At the middle school I do more counseling than in elementary. I do help with testing and I do scheduling for the kids on my grade level. At elementary school I have car rider duty, sorting books for the book drive (all year long), 18 classrooms to do guidance with on a rotating schedule and I am only there three days a week. I never get to see individuals because there is not time and only get to hold groups during student lunchtimes.

I don't think there is much understanding or consideration of counselor's responsibilities or role within school settings, public, charter, or private. I have worked in all of these settings and found they were completely unrealistic in their expectations and no one seemed to even want to sit down and talk about this untenable dilemma for the counselor, day after day and year after year. How is it that the emotional and social needs of our children have been put at the bottom of our educational leadership's list of important goals in the education of our youth? I would like to brainstorm with you ideas for being proactive to change this downward spiral of our professional role and the unraveling of stressed young people with whom we interact daily.

The angst comes from striving to do what is our training, but being confronted with subbing, doing twice as many duties as teachers, having 250 children, not the 30 teachers have, and being used as a "crisis manager" rather than fellow collaborator to pro-actively address student issues. . . . I know lots of counselors who are looking for jobs, and so there is a real fear for job security in standing up to administrators who think we are expendable. I know even with my 20+ years post-masters experience, that thought has crossed my mind more than once.

Secretary of Education Arne Duncan[7] speaks to the cause of low morale of these counselors who want to counsel by suggesting that many high school counselors spend most of their days on nonguidance tasks like being hallway monitors, mailing deficiency reports, filling in as substitute teachers, and administering discipline. Meanwhile, our students desperately need help.

Blaming principals for requiring counselors to provide nonguidance and noncounseling activities and to neglect personal counseling and intervention is only half the story. Counselors themselves have to share much of the blame for taking on a dominantly administrative role and accepting it as their number-one priority while abandoning their personal counseling responsibilities. And education leaders who stress that college admissions should be the number-one role of guidance counselors also share the blame for counselors being trapped in this quasi-administrative role. Here's an example.

The Education Trust, in their report, "Poised to Lead: How School Counselors Can Drive College and Career Readiness,"[8] state that many principals don't recognize the essential role school counselors could have in making sure that the school is equitably preparing students for success after high school. Many principals assign noncounseling duties, from standardized-test coordination to student discipline and substitute teaching, and keep counselors from taking leadership in the school. Saddled with menial tasks, school counselors become quasi-administrators, not agents of equity.

The report suggests that both individual principals and the programs that prepare them need to do some serious thinking about the role of school counselors and how principals can better support their participation in school efforts to solidly prepare all students for what awaits them after high school. Counselors get off blame-free in this assessment of why they are stuck in a role saddled with menial tasks. Many have chosen to go along to get along.

However, the Education Trust report is very critical in other aspects of their work. The report states that counselors themselves can diminish their scope of influence. For example, the report states that in a misguided effort too many counselors allow students to drop rigorous courses or, worse, to never enroll in them. Unfortunately, this bless-your-heart mentality results in choices that slam the doors on these students' futures. It excuses them from doing hard work, a practice that has devastating repercussions in limiting their life options. Even when counselors take on their quasi-administrative role, they get criticized.

The report hits hardest with its criticism of counselors with an overemphasis on personal counseling. It states that even school counselors who have high expectations for their students can easily find themselves spending the bulk of their time providing personal and social counseling to individual students. The report suggests that these counselors mean well but the hard truth is that our public schools are not set up to provide therapy to students.

Certainly, when personal and social issues significantly interfere with learning, school counselors need to help. They can best assist students, not with long-term, time-consuming sessions but with brief, short-term counseling sessions, referrals to small-group counseling, or other support systems within the school or community.

Finally, the report suggests that waiting for counselor-student ratios to go down in order to make more time for individual students is not an option. Counselors have to choose. If they opt to wait until ratios improve before tackling the challenge of getting all their students ready, they'll likely be waiting a long time, leaving many of their students on the economic sidelines. Our hope is that far more will do what our top professionals do— collaborate creatively with parents and institutions in the community to prepare every student for college, no matter what.

We see in the assessment and recommendation for the work of counselors why there is such confusion in their ranks. As one counselor said, "I don't know whether I am coming or going, if I am a fish or a fowl."

Reports like this only increase the role confusion of counselors and offer suggestions that don't offer new models for change. The authors of this report tend to focus on problematic issues that they observe and suggest remedies that are in their own self-interest. Their remedies are vague in nature and avoid any critique of the failure of the delivery system that counselors themselves are experiencing and concrete suggestions on how the system can be improved.

Here are some examples of blaming without a helpful response:

- Blaming school principals for giving counselors too many menial, non-counseling tasks to do but simply suggesting that principals need to sit down with their graduate-school mentors to encourage them to better prepare principals for a much broader role for counselors. What this response lacks is suggestions, action plans, and models for principals to use skilled counselors in other, more proactive ways.
- Blaming counselors for failing to stress academic rigor for students and providing an easy way out for them when they do enroll in demanding classes. This charge suggests a picture of lazy counselors taking on a role similar to that of lax parents who let able kids drift into taking easy classes and ruining their chances for a college education. There are other forces and decision-makers in students' lives that have much more influence than counselors—peers, parents, impoverished home situations that require students to work part time, being locked in a failure cycle that leaves them unmotivated, etc. Counselors may have their faults but allowing students an easy pass to avoid academic rigor isn't one of them.
- Blaming some counselors for using too much of their time on personal counseling interventions and offering suggestions such as shorter counseling sessions and referrals to community mental-health agencies. Missing in this suggestion is awareness about the lives of high school students and their schools. Many kids come to school with a host of academic, social, and well-being problems. Schools and counselors are well-placed to intervene to help them. Unfortunately, many counselors see their roles as quasi-administrative and are not available to help troubled students. Some try because of their training and mission to be of help to students. The milieu they work in is not a mental-health clinic or therapist's office where things are orderly and times for sessions are set. Schools have different settings, with daily crises that disrupt scheduling for the counseling of troubled students.
- Suggesting counselors get with the program by urging them to collaborate creatively with parents and institutions in the community to prepare every student for college and career no matter what. What does "collaborate creatively" mean to counselors working in the real school world? What is needed are concrete ideas and plans, not vague suggestions such as "collaborate creatively."

Researcher Denise Beesley,[9] in reviewing the Education Trust's recommendations for the transformation of school-counselor education and training to maximize their counseling services and ensure that the profession keeps pace with societal changes and demands, says that foremost among the trust's observations is that current training programs do not adequately provide counselors with the knowledge and skills they need to be effective. They also emphasize that counselors in the twenty-first century should serve as advocates, leaders, team members, and consultants to students, parents, principals, and community agencies to ensure the academic success of all students.

The Education Trust and Beesley's review give little attention to the specific knowledge and skills counselors need to be effective and just how counselors can serve as advocates, leaders, team members, and consultants in the present, out-of-date delivery system they now work in. This report is nothing more than a vague call for new counselor roles that lacks the necessary specifics on how to reorganize the present guidance and counseling system and implement the needed changes. The report is dead in the water as soon as it reaches the schoolhouse door.

It's no wonder that many counselors wonder whether they are fish or fowl and, as Whiston suggested, continue to do everything and try to manage multiple responsibilities with an overwhelming caseload. They are criticized in some quarters for not doing enough personal counseling and in others, such as the Education Trust report, for doing too much personal counseling at the expense of counseling for the college-bound.

Many counselors are tired of the battles that rage around them and experts telling them to do this or do that to regain their once-lofty place in the school hierarchy with the advent of the large comprehensive high schools of the 1950s. They are like their troubled students, looking for an open door to get the help they desperately need and instead finding only advice—study more, try harder, stop hanging around with that bad crowd, save yourself before it's too late.

As in the Education Trust report, counselors get a lot of advice but no real road map to follow. The report subtly describes the divisions in our high schools that work to create two different worlds for students, one for high-achieving students who get the guidance help to get into competitive colleges and the other for low-achieving, troubled students who can't seem to figure out who they are and how they'll find the pathway to normalcy and success. Counselors are stuck between these two worlds, trying to help each group but lacking a system that can make the connection between the two and bring them together as one diverse helping community, one in which each member cares about and helps the others.

The following are some examples of issues that are dividing our high school communities and that need to be healed before we can be successful in forming a unified community concerned with each person's well-being:

- principals' need for counselors' organizational assistance versus some counselors' needs for an increase in personal counseling roles;
- bright, college-bound students who demand more college-prep counseling versus troubled students who are in need of more personal counseling;

- counselors who see themselves as quasi-administrators versus counselors who see themselves as experts in offering intervention to troubled students;
- high-achieving students seeking rigorous academic courses versus so-called lazy students looking for a way to avoid rigorous academic courses;
- successful, well-behaved students versus failing, acting-out students;
- parents of high-achieving students demanding college-prep courses versus parents of failing students who live at the margins of school life; and
- teachers who feel the school should always work to increase academic rigor versus teachers who feel there is already too much pressure on students to succeed and that this pressure is unhealthy and can cause emotional, social, and well-being problems.

It's no mystery as to what kind of counseling services win out in divided school communities. It's obvious who the winners are who get the majority of counselors' time and intervention in this outdated counseling model. They are the following:

- high-achieving students encouraged to enroll in rigorous academic courses;
- high-achieving students and their parents who demand college-prep counseling;
- teachers of rigorous academic courses who pressure counselors to enroll high-achieving students in their classes;
- high-achieving students who provide good-news-only stories to demonstrate the school's successes; and
- principals who need some members of the counseling staff to take over administrative duties.

And it's no mystery who the losers are in this system, who receive a relatively small or no amount of counselors' time and intervention. They are the following:

- counselors well-trained to intervene and help students headed toward the margins of school life;
- troubled and failing students who need intervention;
- parents of troubled and failing students who need intervention for their children and their families; and
- teachers who are child-centered, as well as lobby administrators and counselors who support increased personal counseling to help students with emotional, social, and well-being problems that negatively impact their academic achievement.

How do counselors find their place and bring these divisive groups together as one? Maybe Dr. Seuss has some advice when he says,

> When you you're in a slump, you're not much fun. Un-slumping yourself if not easily done. You'll come to a place where the streets are not marked. Some windows are lighted. But mostly they're darked. Do you dare stay out? Do you dare to go in? How much can you lose? How much can you win? Simple it's not, I'm afraid you will find, for a mind-maker-upper to make up his mind. You can get so confused that you'll start to race, headed, I fear, toward a most useless place. The Waiting Place, for people just waiting. [10]

That's where most counselors live out their professional lives—in a waiting place for another chance, another place in which their work can be valued again, an escape from a failed workplace not of their own making.

In many high schools, caring and skilled counselors are trying to figure out how to proceed to adjust their programs and stay current. The difficulty I have observed in this process lies not with new ideas but with escaping from the old ones. Many seem reluctant and unsure about grasping that there is a huge need in today's high schools to raise their minimum personal counseling role to a higher level, to make sure they have the necessary training and demonstrate that they are up to the task.

They have for too long presented themselves to their building principals as junior administrators and have been gladly willing to take on the activities associated with this role. They've sold their bosses and the public that they are in the administrator club and have an administrative persona, not a counselor persona. Today's times require a changed persona, and that means moving, albeit slowly, out of an often 100-percent administrative role into adding a personal counseling element, demonstrating that when it comes to personal and social development, they are players.

Picture a high school graduation in which the director of guidance describes for parents how many students were helped to succeed by members of the counseling staff, citing example after example of students who came back from the margins of school life and graduated because a caring and skilled counselor made a commitment to help and stay the course with these students.

Counselors have to face the hard reality that they are being blamed for the problems of the old organization and free themselves from this failed system. That means showing in every school and community forum that their personal counseling interventions work and are a needed entity of the school's guidance and counseling program. It's not an add-on that has no priority.

People have to visualize what change means and see that the change has something in it for them and needs to be valued. Counselors have to speak clearly and passionately about the kids they help, tell their stories so administrators, teachers, students, parents, school board members, and community residents grasp the value of their interventions.

Members of the school community and the public can relate to stories of kids who succeed against all odds, success stories of personal struggles, and stories of caring educators who take notice of kids in need and make it their business to help make the change everyone can relate to and embrace. It's a process of personalizing why, how, and when counselors are social and developmental specialists.

This process is positive in nature and moves in a new direction rather than the counselors digging in their heels and defending their present out-of-date system. They need to be about defending their profession, what they do to help members of the school community. That is best done by highlighting stories of their helping work to everyone in the school and community who now questions the role and value of counselors; highlighting stories of real interventions puts a face on how the process works.

It helps make administrators, teachers, students, parents, citizens, and fellow counselors aware of the lives of troubled teens, their struggle to change, the troubled lives many lead outside of school, and the new hope that they can choose a new path and be free of addiction and be successful students for the first time in their school lives. Real stories of successful interventions serve as an important educational tool to sell uninformed and resisting members of the school community on the need to have quick, skilled intervention ready and set when trouble visits any member of the school community.

This documentation of a successful intervention is critical to the revamping of the counselor organization. Too often counselors focus on numbers and data to show their value: college acceptances, test scores, attendance, a decrease in discipline problems, etc. The real stories of how students, parents, staff members, and even administrators are helped by personal counseling interventions are often absent. Chapter 6 documents a successful intervention program and suggests why we need to build a library that documents other successful intervention programs.

The stories are there and need to be mined for the value they bring to students, parents, staff, administrators, and counselors. There are many examples of good-news intervention stories that are being overshadowed by the get-to-college-only news. These stories need to see the light of day so every member of the school community becomes aware of the important work of counselors who are freed up and expected to do personal counseling.

NOTES

1. William L. Fibkins, *An Educator's Guide to Understanding the Personal Side of Students' Lives* (Lanham, MD: Rowman & Littlefield, 2003), 29–49.

2. James B. Conant, *The American High School Today: A First Report to Interested Citizens* (New York: McGraw-Hill, 1959).

3. James B. Conant, *The Comprehensive High School: A Second Report to Interested Citizens* (New York: McGraw-Hill, 1967).

4. Carol Dahir and Carolyn B. Stone, "School Counselor Accountability: The Path to Social Justice and Systemic Change," *Journal of Counseling and Development* 87 (winter 2009): 12–20.

5. Susan C. Whiston, "Response to the Past, Present, and Future of School Counseling: Some Issues," *Professional School Counseling* 5, no. 3 (February 2002): 148–55.

6. Linkedin.com, Online discussion by members of the School Counselor Network group (accessed March 15, 2012).

7. U.S. Department of Education, "The Three Myths of High School Reform: Secretary Arne Duncan Remarks at the College Board AP Conference," July 15, 2010, www.ed.gov/news/speeches/three-myths-high-school-reform-secretary-arne-duncans-remarks-college-board-ap-confere (accessed March 21, 2013).

8. The Education Trust, "Poised to Lead: How School Counselors Can Drive College and Career Readiness," The Education Trust, December 2011, pp. 1–8, available online at www.cadfacte.net/poised-to-lead-how-school-counselors-can-drive-college-and-career-readiness (accessed March 21, 2013).

9. Denise Beesley, "Teachers' Perceptions of School Counselor Effectiveness: Collaborating for Student Success," *Education* 125, no. 2 (winter 2005): 259.

10. Dr. Seuss, *Oh, the Places You'll Go!* (New York: Random House, 1990), 20–21.

Chapter Three

A Profession in Search of a Model for Change

Offering Only Solutions That Are Not Really Solutions

The focus of this chapter is on the good intentions of counselor leaders to make the necessary changes in high school counseling programs. The current delivery system is crippled by assigning counselors to help students either by grade level or alphabetically instead of assigning counselors based on their skills to help specific student groups in the school. A new delivery system is needed. For example, in our large high schools why not assign counselors based on their skills to the following areas?

- individual and group counseling for students, parents, and staff;
- scheduling students for class;
- college admissions and scholarships;
- mandated testing;
- career counseling; and
- discipline counseling.

This differentiated staffing model works best in large high schools where a number of counselors are available. Many of these counselors do prefer the quasi-administrative counseling role that comes with college admissions, scheduling, testing, discipline, and career counseling. However, in many high schools there are well-trained counselors itching to carry out an individual- and group-counseling role plus training teachers and advisors, parents, and students as peer helpers, and serving as an advisor to principals who are in need of a trusted advisor to keep them updated on student problems and issues.

However, the good ideas and intentions of counselor leaders to change the way counselor work is arranged will never see the light of day unless counselors are deployed based on student needs and the specific skills of counselors who meet their needs. Here's an example of how staff resources are deployed in the military to win battles and wars. Talent and skills come first in assigning personnel to critical segments of the corps, such as:

- intelligence;
- medical;
- reconnaissance;
- food and supplies;
- plane pilots;
- mechanics;
- transportation;
- weapons and armor;
- construction;
- leadership;
- support;
- prisoner control;
- burial; and
- training.

Specialization is required for success, and expertise on behalf of the corps needs to be homegrown and supportive to make sure all operations are ready and set to go. The risks and consequences of poorly trained or inept soldiers in war come at a great price. Soldiers die or get badly injured, and defeat is always close at hand when the core has members who are not up to the task, not unlike a baseball team that may be playing with a few all stars but that also has a number of players who are mediocre and weak links.

The difference is in war, soldiers die when some of their colleagues are weak links when the battle starts. In baseball the consequences are less drastic: losing games, failing to reach the playoffs, never winning a world championship as long as the weak players remain on the field.

And that scenario is very true for students who are in need of specific kinds of intervention and find themselves assigned to a counselor who lacks the counseling skills to help them. In this scenario, students may not die or get wounded as in war because they find themselves in the wrong place without support, but they can die emotionally and fade away toward the margins of school life because the helper assigned to help them is a weak link and not up to the task.

Deploying counselors with specific skills to offer is critical to the academic and personal success of every student. Think of this model as the shopping-mall model in which students can walk into many doors to get help from expert counselors in the area of their need. Here's an example of some of the shopping-mall counseling services with bright lights to illuminate their offering:

- personal counseling;
- college-admission and scholarship counseling;
- mandated testing;
- scheduling for classes;
- career counseling;
- discipline counseling; and
- training and consultation.

This shopping-mall process with many open doors requires that counselors rethink what skills they bring to the table and how best they can help students and members of the school community given their interest and skills—that is, creating an environment in which they are best able to serve as a strong team player, not a weak link.

This model with its clear pathways for help is a win-win model not only for counselors but also for building principals, as it gives them a clear idea of "what counselors do" and how each component in this model is valuable to the overall success of the school—a model that can encourage principals to better understand what kind of counseling helps students, parents, staff, and even themselves. This model gives a reason to avoid assigning counselors to menial tasks and values counselors as key players, not weak links that can't be counted on.

However, change is difficult. Even when people's lives are taking a bad turn and a change is needed, people tend to stay with what they know. That's true for couples whose relationships are falling apart but who tend to stay together for all the obvious reasons, or people involved in an abusive situation where the bruises keep coming but who hang on with the promise that the abuse will stop.

Therefore, it comes as no surprise that counselors, being human, will tend to stay with what they know, and many have done so for years. Many may face an increasing number of critics, but for them it's like hanging on to the old, worn, moth-ridden sweater that needs to be taken to the dump but is kept in the bottom drawer because it represents the good times long past. Comfort zones, even with critics escalating the call for change, can be difficult to change.

As Whiston reminds us,

Counselors continue to do everything. They wonder at the end of the day what they have accomplished. One of the reasons for this is the multiple expectations that people have of school counselors and most counselors' basic desire to help. One of the strengths of school counselors is their dedication and willingness to "pitch in" and help. This strength is also a weakness, for many counselors try to manage multiple responsibilities and overwhelming caseloads the best they can. This "make do" attitude often results in some responsibilities being neglected because of conflicting expectations and complex duties.[1]

Changing the role that Whiston rightly identifies calls for counselors to begin to reflect on what's abusive about their job: when they have to do everything, wonder at the end of the day what they accomplished, and always have to be ready to "pitch in" and help and make due given all the tasks they are asked to complete successfully .For many counselors, the feeling is being stuck in a broken organization in which they are expected to march on and pull together as a team even though the path continues to be more difficult.

Here's an example of a call for a change in the way counselors are deployed in order to serve the needs of more students. An email to the School Counselors Group on LinkedIn.com by a high school counselor read:

> We're being asked to revamp our counselor configuration, two counselors responsible for attendance, two for scheduling, two for counseling, and one for college/career counseling. Our principal wants us to think out of the box and this is his proposal. We think it is ludicrous but we also want to look at other ways of configuring our counseling caseloads to most benefit our students. We are currently configured alphabetically. Assigning students by grade doesn't work. We are a high school/seven counselors don't split evenly into four grade levels.[2]

The principal is right on with the model for a differentiated staffing pattern with counselors deployed by skills and tasks rather than alphabet or grade, although including attendance counseling as a part of the counselor's job description is a stretch. It really is an administrative task. But the other areas he suggests are very consistent with the differentiated staffing model this book proposes.

Yet the counselor suggests the idea is "ludicrous." And she is supported by one respondent who says:

> I agree. The idea is ludicrous! Categorizing services defies the (ASCA) comprehensive counseling program concept. Have you thought of one counselor remaining with one grade and the other six splitting the remaining three grades by splitting the alphabet, and stay with those students for three years at a time? I suggest you get together and represent your principal with a comprehensive counseling program that allows each of you to provide services individually as well as collaboratively.

Another respondent says, "I add my vote to the ludicrous part. I've worked in multiple environments and this sounds like the craziest! What about the 'whole person' concept in the ASCA model. Plus, each counselor will lose their own broader professional skills. I certainly hope the person who dreamt this up was not a counselor at some point."

And another says, "The major issue for me in this plan would be the two counselors assigned to counseling in your principal's model would certainly be emotionally saturated. That's an exhausting role to be assigned exclusively."

This is a taste of how counselors often respond to any suggestions that they are assigned to students by skills rather than alphabet or grade level. What are these counselors suggesting beyond the notion that it is ludicrous, and what do these remarks reveal about their expected and welcomed resistance?

Here are some answers that challenge their responses:

"I suggest you present your principal with a comprehensive counseling program that allows each of you to provide service individually and collaboratively."

What if some counselors do not possess skills to provide one or more services required for students? Here's what happens in the real school world. Life goes on. Counselors are left to go on no matter how poor their skills are because of lack of supervision, feedback from colleagues who see them as a weak link, and lack of interest and motivation to learn new skills on their part. Here's a sports analogy: there is little thought about putting the ball in the hands of the counselors who can best get the job done and taking the ball out of the hands of those counselors who can't or who refuse to get the job done.

Kids suffer when their counselors are expected to deliver help but in reality don't. They may talk a good game but they are the absent helpers. The kids are being deprived but often silenced. Looking the other way is their response. Counselors are not made equally. Some are better than others and need to be deployed where they are needed to help kids. Those that are not skilled helpers need to be deployed to quasi-administrative tasks and need to stop simply pretending to help but not delivering.

"Each counselor will lose their own broader professional skills. I certainly hope the person who dreamt this up was not a counselor."

But what does losing "their own broader professional skills" mean? All counselors are not equal. Some have skills and talents in personal counseling, while others have talents and skills in college counseling, scheduling, testing, etc. And there are other counselors who lack skills in general. The hiring of counselors is often a political process and is one way to move up an inept teacher, pay off a winning coach, or place a close friend or relative in a favored school position—weak links who don't have many skills, just friends in high places who are members of the good-old-boy network.

These are the counselors who resist any change process aimed at moving well-trained and skilled counselors into places where real skill is lacking. Differentiated staffing may not be the miracle cure for the counseling professional, but it recognizes and awards skilled counselors and pushes deadwood counselors into roles where they are less likely to stymie the hopes and dreams of kids.

"The major issue for me would be that the two counselors assigned to counseling would certainly be emotionally saturated. That's an exhausting role to be assigned exclusively."

Any school professional, whether he or she is a teacher, administrator, or counselor, who works intensively with students will find it a demanding role. You put in your dues to make sure the students you are responsible for are helped and well prepared for what life's challenges will bring them. We need professionals who are energetic, physically and emotionally reading, and motivated to go into the lion's den and mix it up with their students and win them over.

We do not need professionals who fear being emotionally saturated or exhausted. That comes with the territory and is a necessary part of delivering one's best on our student's behalf, particularly the ones who resist us the most and are tough—tough characters who want us to ignore them , go away, and leave them be. We owe it to these students to take them on and deliver the help they need. It's easy not to listen, to avoid tough kids, to look for kids who are easy to help, and to stay in our comfort zone. As the one young counselor said to his older mentor, "How come you don't look tired after listening to kids' problems all day?" The older mentor replied, "Who listens?"

The problem counselors face is not about the American School Counselor Association's national model, which I will describe in the next chapter, but about recognizing counselors that are not equal and as a result are not up to handling successfully all the services they are being required to deliver. As Whiston suggested in this paradigm, something has to give and some responsibilities are neglected because of conflicting expectations.

What is needed is a recognition of the skills available to school guidance and counseling departments, which counselors are best prepared to delivery these skills, what training is needed to maintain a high level of skills, and a shift of low-performing counselors into roles where they can take care of quasi-administrative duties and be moved far away from counseling students on critical academic, social, and emotional needs. Put simply, low-performing counselors should be put out to pasture where they can do no harm and maybe a little good.

NOTES

1. Susan C. Whiston, "Response to the Past, Present, and Future of School Counseling: Some Issues," *Professional School Counseling* 5, no. 3 (February 2002): 148–55.

2. LinkedIn.com, Online discussion by members of the School Counselor Network group (assessed March 15, 2012).

Chapter Four

The Profession Is Not Dead Yet

Getting Some Help from the American School Counselor Association National Model

This chapter's focus has two goals. One is to review some of the good works of counselors, leaders in beginning a change process to prepare counselors for a leadership role in today's schools. And the second is to review the work that needs to be done if the good ideas and intentions offered if this change process are to succeed. How counselors are deployed is a critical piece.

Let's begin with a review of the American School Counselor Association (ASCA) national model.[1] This model represents the heart and soul of the change process. Here are some suggestions offered in the ASCA executive summary of the model.

School counseling programs are collaborative efforts benefiting students, parents, teachers, administrators, and the overall community. School counseling programs should be an integral part of students' daily educational environment, and school counselors should be partners in student achievement. Unfortunately, school counseling has lacked a consistent identity from state to state, district to district, and even school to school.

This has led to a misunderstanding of what school counseling is and what it can do for a school. As a result, school counseling programs are often viewed as ancillary programs instead of a crucial component to student achievement, and school counselors have not been used to their fullest.

The question has often been posted, "What do school counselors do?" The more important question is, "How are students different because of what school counselors do?"

To help answer this question, the ASCA created *The ASCA National Model: A Framework for School Counseling Programs*. By implementing a

school counseling program based on the ASCA national model, schools and
school districts can:

- establish the school counseling program as an integral component of the
  academic mission of the school;
- ensure that every student has equitable access to the school counseling
  program;
- identify and deliver the knowledge and skills all students should acquire;
  and
- ensure that the school counseling program is comprehensive in design and
  is delivered systematically to all students.

The ASCA national model supports the school's overall mission by promoting academic achievement, career planning, and personal/social development. It serves as a framework to guide states, districts, and individual schools in designing, developing, implementing, and evaluating a comprehensive, developmental, and systematic school counseling program.

The ASCA national model consists of four interrelated components: foundation, delivery system, management system, and accountability.

FOUNDATION

The first component, foundation, dictates how the program is managed and delivered, which in turn leads to the accountability of the program. The information gathered through the accountability process should refine and revise the foundation. Infused throughout the program are the qualities of leadership, advocacy, and collaboration that lead to systemic change.

Historically many school counselors spend much of their time responding to the needs of a small percentage of students, typically those who were high achievers or who were high risk. The ASCA's national model outlines a program allowing school counselors to direct services to every student.

As educators who are specially trained in childhood and adolescent development, school counselors can take a leadership role in effecting systemic change in a school. However, a successful school counseling program is a collaboration of parents, students, school counselors, administrators, teachers, student services personnel, and support staff working together for the benefit of every student.

The ASCA National Model: A Framework for School Counseling Programs keeps the development of the total student at the forefront of the education movement and forms the needed bridge between counseling and education.

The foundation component of the ASCA model includes the beliefs and philosophy that guide the program; the mission, program purpose; and the three student-outcome domains of academic, personal/social, and career development. Collectively these create the core of the school counseling program. According to *The ASCA National Model: A Framework for School Counseling Programs*, the assumptions that form the foundation upon which the school counseling program rests include the following:

A school counseling program:

- reaches every student;
- is comprehensive in scope;
- is preventative in design;
- is developmental in nature;
- is an integral part of the total educational program for student success;
- selects measurable student competencies based on local need in the areas of academic, career, and personal/social domains;
- has a delivery system that includes school guidance curriculum, individual planning, responsive services, and system support;
- is implemented by a credentialed school counselor;
- is conducted in collaboration with all stakeholders;
- uses data to drive program decisions;
- monitors student progress;
- measures both process and outcome results and analyzes critical data elements; and
- shares successes with stakeholders.

DELIVERY SYSTEM

The school counseling program's delivery system includes the activities, interactions, and areas in which counselors work to deliver the program. Within the delivery system there are four components: school counseling curriculum, individual student planning, responsive services, and system support. The school counseling curriculum provides a vehicle for delivering information and connecting with every student in a systematic way.

Individual student planning involves working with students and their families to develop and implement the student's individual learning plan directed toward identifying and achieving future academic and career goals. Responsive services address student's direct, immediate concerns and include counseling, consultation, and referral. Finally, the system-support component enables the school counseling program to be effective through a variety of support activities including professional development, consultation, collaboration, learning, program management, and operations.

MANAGEMENT SYSTEM

The management of school counseling programs is an organized effort: concrete, clearly delineated, and reflective of the school site's needs. It involves analysis of relevant data, development of action plans to meet objections, and provision of organizational activities. It answers the questions of when and why certain activities will take place, who will implement them, and on what authority the school counseling program is delivered. Clear expectations and purposeful interaction with all stakeholders result in a school counseling program that is integrated into the total educational program, and that provides student growth and development.

ACCOUNTABILITY

The key question, "How are students different as a result of the school counseling program?," is answered within the context of the accountability system. School counselors determine the effectiveness of the comprehensive school counseling program by measuring results, and they use that information to inform program improvement. By collecting data, especially around changes in students' knowledge, skills, and dispositions, the school counselor can evaluate the program's impact on student achievement, graduation rates, attendance, disciplinary referrals, and other student and system outcomes.

School counselors have many duties and responsibilities related to designing and implementing a comprehensive school counseling program. Therefore, programs should free school counselors to do what they do best and what only they can do. Most school counselors have a master's degree and have formal training in both mental health and education. Although school counselors are team players who understand fair-share responsibilities within a school system, they cannot be fully effective when they are taken away from essential counseling tasks to perform noncounseling activities, such as:

- Master schedule duties: In many schools, the function of building the school's master schedule is performed by a school counselor instead of an administrator, when this is clearly an administrative role. School counselors need to participate as consultants and experts in the process, but when they are required to carry the bulk of the responsibility in this area, their ability to provide school counseling services for students is diminished.
- Test coordinating: In a world of increased high-stakes testing, more and more school counselors are called upon to assist in the preparation for testing. The appropriate role for a school counselor is to interpret the

results of these tests and to analyze them in conjunction with multiple measures of student achievement.

• Detention-room coverage: In the absence of a teacher or other certified staff, school counselors often are called upon to cover detention rooms. Their more appropriate role is to assist in appropriate and systemic preventive measures that improve overall behavior and deter attendance in the detention room.

• Discipline: School counselors are not disciplinarians and do not possess the appropriate credentials for disciplining students. Their appropriate role is to provide counseling for students before and/or after discipline, to determine the causes of students' behavior leading to disciplinary action, to develop and deliver schoolwide curriculum for the deterrence of behaviors leading to disciplinary action, and to collaborate on school leadership teams to create policies promoting appropriate behavior on campus.

• Classroom coverage: School counselors understand the need to assist when emergencies arise and classrooms need coverage. Problems arise when school counselors are regularly first in line to cover classes. This is an inappropriate use of counselors' time and skills.

• Clerical responsibilities: School counseling programs require clerical assistance to perform functions outside the school counselors' appropriate job description. Many districts employ guidance assistants to provide this service so school counselors can spend their time in direct service to students.

Although school counselors should be involved in many aspects of students' education, certain non–school counseling tasks should be eliminated or reassigned, if possible, so school counselors can use their skills and knowledge to focus on students' needs. A fine line sometimes separates appropriate from inappropriate activities.

Inappropriate (noncounseling) activities include:

• registering and scheduling all new students;
• administering cognitive, aptitude, and achievement tests;
• signing excuses for students who are tardy or absent;
• performing disciplinary actions;
• sending home students who are not appropriately dressed;
• teaching classes when teachers are absent;
• computing grade-point averages;
• maintaining student records;
• supervising study halls;
• clerical record-keeping; and
• assisting with duties in the principal's office.

Appropriate (counseling) responsibilities include:

- working with one student at a time in a therapeutic, clinical mode;
- designing individual student academic programs;
- interpreting cognitive, aptitude, and achievement tests;
- counseling students with excessive tardiness or absenteeism;
- counseling students with disciplinary problems;
- counseling students about appropriate school dress;
- collaborating with teachers to present guidance curriculum lessons;
- analyzing grade-point averages in relationship to achievement;
- interpreting student records;
- providing teachers with suggestions for better study-hall management;
- ensuring that records are maintained in accordance with state and federal regulations;
- assisting the school principal with identifying and resolving student issues, needs, and problems; and
- collaborating with teachers to present proactive, prevention-based guidance curriculum lessons.

This is an excellent model to serve as a beginning point for overhauling the nation's guidance and counseling system. One can strongly disagree with some "appropriate counseling responsibilities" such as counseling students about appropriate dress and providing teachers with suggestions for better study-hall management, which are considered as being in the realm of administrators. However, overall, it's a move in the right direction.

In particular, the inclusion of "responsive services" is necessary—services that address students' direct, immediate concerns and include counseling, consultation, and referral and "system support," components that enable the school counseling program to be effective through a variety of support activities including professional development, consultation, collaboration, teaming, program management, and operations.

The problem of getting counselors on board this national model is not the intent and hoped-for outcomes but rather the freeing-up of the present guidance and counseling workforce to successfully carry out some of the components of the "delivery system" such as "responsive services" and "system support," which include counseling, consultation, referral, training, collaboration, and professional development.

Why? Researchers Dilani M. Perera-Diltz and Kimberly L. Mason in "Ideal to Real: Duties Performed by School Counselors"[2] provide some insight into what counselors feel they are comfortable delivering, not necessarily what the ASCA report is recommending that they need to do. Their assessment of a survey of 1,704 elementary, middle school, junior high, and high school counselors informs the extent to which the school counselors perform duties that are not endorsed by the profession.

For example, the greatest variation across building levels was in scheduling duties performed by school counselors with almost 90 percent endorsement from high school counselors who also endorsed testing more than their counterparts at other building levels. Perera-Diltz and Mason suggest that other research indicates high school counselors engage more in nonendorsed duties because of the following reasons:

- their school principals believe counselors should supervise hall duty, bus loading and unloading, and lunch duty and spend time testing students;
- staff shortages due to budget cuts and lack of funds may influence duties assigned to counselors; and
- school counselors may volunteer their time to engage in nonendorsed duties due to the needs of school and/or personal comfort in performing these services.

As Andrew V. Beal[3] suggests, a major difficulty in program implementation with counselors is the pressure on them to perform noncounseling duties, activities such as record-keeping, registration and scheduling of new students, coordinating or administering achievement tests, teaching classes when teachers are absent, computing grade-point averages, master schedule development, and sending students home who are not appropriately dressed.

However, instead of finding ways to demonstrate to building principals that counselors can deliver the counseling services that students, parents, staff, and administrators need in what Robert Bardwell describes as "today's complex school environment,"[4] what usually happens, and what has been a repeated pattern over the years, is for some counselor leaders to plea for additional counselors. Bardwell, director of guidance at Monson High School in Monson, Massachusetts, and an officer in the New England Association of College Admissions days, falls into this trap of making the ritual pleas for more counselors, counselors who are not going to be hired in these tough economic times. Here is what he says:

> If school counselors were used in more effective ways, and if there were more school counselor's to help our students, then our graduation rates and college-going races would improve and our student would be better prepared to overcome the numerous obstacles standing in the way of their success. The percentage of students bound for higher education increase when they have access to highly trained school counselors who are not at lunch duty, completing paperwork or counting test booklets.
>
> And it does not help that most adults do not know what school counselors do, did not have a good experience with their school counselor or are not even aware that they have access to one while in school. The recent report in the

spring 2010: Can I Get a Little Advice Here "does not help our image." We need more funding and attention paid to school counselors. The bottom line is that the school counselor of today is not the guidance counselor of yesterday. We are much better prepared and improved model. Give us a chance to prove our worth and I guarantee our students will be better as a result. The solution is clear but is anyone who is in a position to avert the crises paying much attention?

Bardwell may well lament that people don't know what counselors do, and some counselors are shuttled into noncounseling duties such as lunch duty, paperwork, and arranging test booklets, and recent reports suggest that students do not have a good experience with their counselors. However, he says, "Today's counselors are much better prepared than their counterparts from the past." He asks for the profession to be given a chance to prove its worth along with more funding and attention paid to counselors and their worth.

As these examples from a counselor in the field suggest, the good idea and intentions put forth by the ASCA recommendations are being met with resistance from some counselors, many at the high school level, who still focus and support their role in noncounseling duties, and other counselor leaders like Bardwell who suggest that the public doesn't understand how much good counselors do and that all they need is a chance to show their worth so that more counselors can be hired.

There is a lot of blame going on, especially aimed at principals for not using counselors effectively, a lack of funding, and counselors assigned to noncounseling duties, and pleas for more counselors being ignored by those in a position to avert the crisis is looming over the profession.

But where is the call from counselors in the field for how to sell their principals, staff, student, parents, and community members on their worth? Where does the blaming stop and efforts begin to demonstrate where, how, and when counselors do make a difference in the lives of students, parents, staff, and administration?

What's missing in the ASCA recommendations is the awareness that many counselors are set in their ways and have developed daily habits that are consistent with quasi-administrative roles. As *New York Times* columnist David Brooks[5] points out, researchers at Duke University calculate that more than 40 percent of the actions we take are governed by habit, not actual decisions.

Researchers have come to understand the structure of habits, cue, and routine reward. The daily routine of most counselors—scheduling students for classes, developing and managing testing programs, college-admission prep, career guidance and counseling, and disciplining acting-out students—are guidance components that lend themselves to rewards and status in the current school hierarchy.

Brooks points out that the habits formed in the lives of professionals are fortified by a yearning like the yearning for admiration. And the components mentioned above are ways of counselors to market themselves and place themselves as indispensable players in selling the school's mission.

As any school reformer knows, changing habits of educators who are set in their ways, comfortable, and insulated from the change process usually doesn't work because they are at the center of the system that needs changing.

When arguments for reform, such as the ASCA national model, arrive at the schoolhouse door, many counselors may say they agree but continue to do the same thing they already know how to do, even more assiduously than before. Long-term habits are burned into their working persona and role. Many of these counselors are not getting aboard the change process offered by the ASCA.

But, thankfully, there are counselors and counselor leaders who do have a new dream for themselves and the future of their profession. And, as a result of these new dreams, a chasm has opened up between those professionals and the organization upon which they depend. They see an organization in decline bolstered up by many of their colleagues who are all too comfortable with their current workplace and the rewards and affirmations it bestows on them.

And as the ASCA leaders and supportive counselors in the field forge ahead, it comes as no surprise that they are being blamed for causing turmoil and conflict among counselors and problems of the old organization when the acts suggest the opposite. The difficulty lies not in new ideas, but in escaping the old ones with suggestions for changing the counselor's workplace.

Yet as Zuboff and Maxmin[6] suggest, letting go of the past is painful. What lies beyond the light of the lamppost? People know how to operate in the system that already exists. They know how to compete and how to succeed in that system. Changing the deep structure of a system is threatening to everyone. There will be new winners and losers, new skills to learn, and new ranking rules. These fears are compounded by the fact that many people have invested their entire career in the old structures. Change can belittle their lifetime achievements. It can also diminish all that they have sacrificed.

And, directly to the heart of our discussion, Zuboff and Maxmin say another reason why people evade deep structure changes involves the relationships and commitments that people have developed both inside and outside the system. Individuals frequently find it hard to change because they are afraid of disappointing the people closest to them such as marital partners or professional colleagues. If a person has been valued by important others, he tends to fear the loss of that positive regard if he undergoes change and possibly develops new directions. Peer pressure to stay tied to old, out-of-date ways of doing business is a powerful weapon employed by resisting counselors to keep counselors bent on change under control.

However, there is growing demand for counselors to demonstrate their value to the education system. One of the major recommendations for change in the guidance and counseling profession centers on the word *accountability*, that is, making the role and tasks of counselors abundantly clear for counselors themselves, building principals, teachers, students, parents, and taxpayers. This stated goal tends to raise the resistance of some counselors who have, as Carola A. Dahir and Carolyn B. Stone[7] suggest, used time-on-task and report totals to demonstrate accountability. They suggest that counting services is not accountability as defined by the No Child Left Behind Act. Task and time analysis does not show any relationship to impacting student achievement and is perceived as a defense mechanism to account for productivity.

Instead, as Dahir and Stone point out, the ASCA recommendations emphasize annual school report cards publicizing critical data elements such as attendance, demographics, graduation, postsecondary planning rates, and standardized testing results, for example, putting into place school-improvement goals based on the percentage of students making improvements in such areas as:

- improved attendance;
- reducing school failure;
- reducing retentions;
- reducing discipline incidents;
- improving grades;
- increased rates of students graduating;
- increased rate of students attending postsecondary school;
- increased PSAT scores; and
- improved test scores.

This is a good plan but it lacks a critical component that would make it a winner: the recommendation to do away with the long-time practice of assigning counselors by alphabet or grade, rather than skills and abilities, a system that is much alive in our secondary school, a system that is a poor use of the skill of staff and directly responsible for the problems paralyzing guidance programs and the demise of the counseling role of counselors. We need a new model for assigning counselors—for example, assigning counseling staff by (1) counselors who have an interest, skill, and commitment to offer individual- and group-counseling intervention and provide ongoing training for them and (2) counselors who prefer college admissions, scheduling, and related quasi-administrative work.

This is a model that can bring the counseling and quasi-administrative camp together as allies, valued teammates, both doing what they do well. With this differentiated staffing model, guidance counselors can offer teens and parents the help they need on both personal and academic fronts, thus restoring the leadership mission of counselors that was embraced in the exciting days of the 1950s but failed to adjust to a world that required a new role for counselors in order to deliver needed services to a changed school community in search of a beacon of hope and support.

What is needed is an intervention model that clearly identifies clear pathways for counseling help for students, parents, staff, and administrators, each of whom can become at risk and headed toward a failure experience in their lives. The bottom can fall out for every member of the school community, and help needs to be offered that is easily available and accessible. Someone has to be accountable for this help.

When personal counseling duties are assigned to specific counselors, they and the intervention process become accountable overnight. These counselors become the face of the intervention process and become known through the school and the community as the "go to" professionals for students in need of help and support. And, in this role, they are ideally positioned to collect observations about the kinds of problems students are confronting in their lives, the counseling interventions that appear to work well, and the kinds of support these students need for caring adults in their lives such as teachers, support staff, coaches, parents, and community members as well as from their fellow students, all allies in the helping process.

These observations are data that can be collected to demonstrate the value of counseling to legislators, school board members, principals, and other stakeholders who are, as Dahir and Stone suggest, pressured to demonstrate improved academic success for every student.

These observations can work to show how peers, teachers, support staff, administrators, parents, and the community activists are collectively partners in the helping process, thereby creating "a circle of wellness" in which no student in the school or community is left without the counseling and support they need now.

Secondary schools can develop such a responsive system that emphasizes both the percentages of student improvement in various components related to academic success *and* selected case studies—for example, case studies of how academic success came to a variety of students who were searching for an open door to find ways to break their failure cycle, case studies that make clear the importance of a tandem approach in which both arms of a counseling department, counselors who are identified as personal counselors and counselors who are quasi-administrators, act together, doing what they do well in support of students, parents, teachers, support staff, and principals.

Demonstrating how personal counseling does help troubled students from a variety of school groups find success serves to refocus leaders of guidance and counseling programs on the important role of personal counseling and so they may accept that personal counseling needs to join the big-five priorities of college admissions, scheduling and course selection, mandated testing, career and vocational counseling, and discipline counseling. And, in the process, they can become aware that their professional lives have often been limited to staying with and accepting old habits, old habits that placed them in a cocoon of comfort, no risks, and rewards based on their outdated quasi-administrative role.

Data from case studies can serve to provide a window into the real lives and issues of students, parents, staff, and administrators. A process in which real stories of students are joined with real stories of counselors who are able to break out of their professional cocoons and take on the new roles asked for in the ASCA model. Examples of students and professionals who go through major changes in their lives successfully can serve as powerful teaching moments and selling points for those who struggle mightily to sustain the status quo. The observations represent the good things that can happen if help is easily available and sustained.

And finally these observations are critical to educating building principals about how the intervention of personal counselors can help students to improve not only their academic and personal lives, but also the lives of parents, teachers, their school, and their community. High school principals are busy, busy people and the pressure on them to maintain a safe school environment, raise academic performance, reduce discipline problems, rid the school of bullying, increase graduation and postsecondary enrollment rates, and increase staff morale is increasing.

This is an extremely difficult job for a principal and a few assistant principals to handle in our large high schools, maybe impossible without credible help and support from members of the school staff, such as counselors and teacher leaders who know their students well and provide an open door for help and contact.

As a result, in most large high schools, principals have little out-of-the-office time to know their students; observe them in class, the hallways, lunch, and activities; and be a positive presence in the school. They have little time to create a presence in which they know each student and the students know them, establishing a positive connection by daily, weekly, ongoing personal contact. In many of our large, overcrowded high schools, principals are locked in their offices trying to figure out how to reduce discipline and suspension rates, ways to increase attendance, test scores, graduation and postsecondary enrollment rates, and increase staff morale in a time when teachers are continually being asked to do more with less.

As a result, they are often isolated from the school world they are leading and miss out on the positive things that are happening with their students, staff, and parents. Yes they can analyze the percentage of students who are becoming better achievers, but they receive far too few real stories of how students at the margins of school life are being helped by caring counselors. As such, many principals, as has been reported previously in this book, view counselors in a negative way and only see their worth as quasi-administrators who in the end do little personal counseling and are always asking for more staff in a time when school budgets are tightening.

However, overwhelmed principals cannot be blamed for their views of counselors. They are too busy holding down the fort amid daily attacks. Rather, it is up to counselors to demonstrate that they are making a positive difference in the lives of students, parents, staff, and even principals themselves. Principals need to be educated about the good things counselors are doing and that education's main thrust needs to be establishing weekly meetings with counselors who are ready and set to share observations, real stories, about how they are successfully intervening and helping students, finding a new pathway to academic and personal success.

There should be a weekly conversation in which counselors present their principals with documents describing the students they are seeing, the problems they present, and their intervention plan. In this way, the principal not only gets to know how the counselor's role is played out in their school, but also has the opportunity to know the faces and real-life struggles of many of his students, a process whose aim is to, for a short time, one class period week, free the principal from his many demands and one that serves to increase personalization for all involved: the principal, counselor, students, and parents.

In this role, the counselor is the messenger, bringing to the principal observations and stories of successful interventions, but also stories of how their interventions with some students and parents are more difficult, failing, but they are not giving up—an intervention system trying to change students one by one, a process that reinforces for their principal that students who get help to overcome the troubles that are holding them back from being successful in academics and their personal lives often increase their attendance, become less disruptive, avoid suspension, increase their grades and test scores, gradate, and attend postsecondary education.

They become doers, participants, and important models for peers stuck in a failure pattern at the margins of school life. Some students need "live" examples of how peers stuck in similar failure patterns found their way out with the help of a caring counselor. These observations of how students changed their lives for the better are then important not only for building principals but also for peers stuck in a similar failure pattern, teachers who observe the positive change in the academic performance and behavior of failing students, and parents of failing students looking for interventions to help their child and themselves.

These observations from counselors of students in search of academic and personal well-being are data that can be used by building principals to determine if the ASCA recommendation for a "responsive service" that "addresses student's direct, immediate concerns and including counseling, consultation and referral" is working well or needs improvement, and if the ASCA recommendation for "system support" that "enables school counseling programs to be effective through a variety of support activities including professional development, consultation, and collaboration" is also working well or needs improvement.

These observations add an important component to the ASCA accountability process because they help educate administrators, school board members, legislators, staff, students, parents, and citizens/taxpayers by showing the positive impact the school counseling program can haves on student achievement and on the goals of the school improvement plan. And it includes recommendations from the Breaking Ranks II report[8] that schools need to go beyond gathering data that is limited to academic improvement of students and include observations about student aspiration, strengths, and weaknesses that may prevent school success. In other words, observations that yield data about the drams and hopes of marginal students and those adults in the school such as counselors who are responsible to help these students' dreams and hopes become reality.

This kind of data helps bring clarity to what happens when the stories of troubled students becomes known in the school. Who is responsible for intervening? What is the plan for intervention? How are critical sources of support such as teachers, school nurses, coaches, support staff, and parents involved in the intervention? How are the data and details, the stories, of the intervention documented and made known to the principal? How is the intervention monitored and how are decisions made relative to referral with a school or community agency?

The path to skilled intervention and the role of every member of the school community—administrators, counselors, teachers, support staff, students, and parents—need to be clearly understood. It requires specific, detailed information on everyone's role when a red flag is raised about students in trouble such as what occurred at Columbine High School, where evidently there were few open doors were at-risk students could be "caught" and saved from committing a violent act. *Education Week* writer Marianne D. Hurst puts the need for skilled intervention in perspective when she quotes Frank DeAngelis from Columbine High School[9] when he says, "The biggest thing that needs to be done nationwide is making sure kids have a place to express themselves and seek help."

This is sound advice from an educator who knows the cost of creating a first-rate academic school organization but not an organization prepared to intervene to address the emotional well-being of some students headed toward the margins of school life and in those shadows finding only isolation, anonymity, and remaining undetected by those charged with seeking out and helping kids before their withdrawal leads to mischief, violence, and tragedy that could have been avoided.

For some students, changes in their lives come much too quickly; a barrage of misfortunes arrive with no let-up. Some children become adults overnight, sometimes forced to take care of siblings while a single parent works or to live with an abusive relative while their parents "get their lives together." Building principals, educated by caring counselors who regularly report observations and data about kids in need and their efforts to help them, are well-positioned and prepared to use this data to educate the entire school community about the costs for students and parents headed toward the margins of school and community life.

Principals should regularly remind educators, support staff, students, parents, and community agencies that when they turn a blind eye, look the other way, feel it's somebody else's domain to intervene, they are missing the chance to help, catch them before they fall. We are our brothers' and sisters' keepers, so prepare yourself to act by knowing who to call in a crisis. And counselors, through their gathering of observations and data about students and parents caught in a failure, can help by offering training to make sure no student is left unattended when trouble strikes.

Personal counselors can have a unique role in the school community as both a documenter and a messenger, serving as a collector and reporter of observation about students' quest for normality, happiness, aspirations, and fitting in as a valued member of the school community. This is a unique role that can add to the ASCA recommendations. Chapter 5 will focus on this documenter, messenger, and reporting role.

Finally, the personal counseling role may help free counselors from the anxiety of where they seem to be headed as a profession. They are moving through a period surrounded by enormously rapid change, a transition from something relatively fixed toward something not yet clear.

NOTES

1. Judy Bowers, Trish Hatch, and American School Counselor Association, *The ASCA National Model: A Framework for School Counseling Programs* (Alexandria, VA: American School Counselor Association, 2005).

2. Dilani M. Perera-Diltz and Kimberly L. Mason, "Ideal to Real: Duties Performed by School Counselors," *Journal of School Counseling* 6, no. 26 (2008).

3. Andrew V. Beale, "Questioning Whether You Have a Contemporary School Counseling Program," *Clearing House* 78, no. 2 (2004): 73–77.

4. Robert Bardwell, "A Plea for More Counselors," *New York Times*, October 25, 2010, available online at http://thechoice.blogs.nytimes.com/2010/10/25/counselor-2/ (accessed March 21, 2013).

5. David Brooks, "The Machiavellian Temptation," *New York Times*, March 2, 2012, p. 25A.

6. Shoshana Zuboff and James Maxmin, *The Support Economy: Why Corporations Are Failing Individuals and the Next Episode of Capitalism* (New York: Viking, 2002), 34-36.

7. Carola A. Dahir and Carolyn B. Stone, "MEASURE-ing Student Success: School Counselor Accountability," *Vistas*, article 57, available online at http://counseling.org/resources/library/vistas/vistas05/vistas05.art57.pdf (accessed March 21, 2013).

8. National Association of Secondary School Principals (NASSP), "Executive Summary of Break Ranks II: Strategies for Leading High School Reform," *NASSP*, 2004, pp. 1–6, available online at www.nassp.org/portals/0/content/47560.pdf (accessed March 21, 2013).

9. Marianne D. Hurst, "Columbine High: Five Years Later," *Education Week*, April 14, 2004, available online at www.edweek.org/ewstory.cfm?slug=31columbine.h23 (accessed January 6, 2012).

Chapter Five

The Personal Counselor as Observer and Reporter of Student Behavior

As Dahir and Stone suggest (as mentioned in chapter 4), the No Child Left Behind Act has raised the accountability bar for everyone including school counselors. Therefore, it should come as no surprise that school counselors, too, are accountable to strategies and document how the school counseling program contributes to closing the achievement gap and supporting student success.

They say school counselors can initiate, develop, and coordinate prevention and intervention systems that are designed to improve the learning success of every student who is experiencing difficultly with challenging academic coursework. Using data provides a solid foundation for school counselors to act on their belief system and assume a leadership role to identify and rectify issues that impact every student's ability to achieve at an expected level.

Dahir and Stone also point out the importance of collaboration in this process by developing partnerships with education professionals. I would add that it's important to create partnerships specifically with teachers, support staff, principals, parents, students, and community members.

The key words in the ASCA recommendations and Dahir and Stone's assessment are accountability, data collection, documentation, collaboration, and responsibility to bring attention to student progress and results. The ASCA recommendations also state that comprehensive school guidance should free counselors to do what they do best and what only they can do. Most school counselors have a master's degree and are typically the only people in school with formal training in both mental health and education.

Therefore, it makes good sense that adding a personal counseling component to the ASCA recommendations and identifying specific counselors who are charged with initiating, developing, and coordinating a prevention and intervention system to improve the learning success of every student introduces the opportunity to observe, assess, and document the kinds of problems students are confronting that are limiting their academic success, the preventions and interventions that appear to be effective, and the value of other helpers such as teachers, support staff, principals, parents, students, and community members in the prevention and intervention process.

In this new role personal counselors are at the center of the helping process and provide important data on the specifics of how the helping process can be effective in freeing students of the problems that are holding back their academic and personal success and how the helping resources of many members of their school community can be brought to bear to contribute and support the intervention process.

In this new paradigm the counselors identified as personal counselors take on a new role not only as a personal counselor but also as an observer, documenter, chronicler, and reporter of just how the intervention process works and what factors contribute to its success. Here's how personal counselors ready themselves for this new role.

Personal counselors are ideally placed to assess and document the problems that students are experiencing that interfere with their academic and personal success. Each day they are involved in situations with troubled students in which they listen to what is happening and try to make sense of what is going on so they can act to guide these students through these troubled times with a minimum of pain and a maximum of growth and learning. Identifying, welcoming, and inviting students involved in a failure cycle into counseling before they give up and find themselves at the margins of school life is a critical part of a school counselor's prevention and intervention role.

But students involved in a failure cycle often resist initial overtures by personal counselors to help them; sometimes these students become less willing to accept "help" and demands from school authorities that they change their ways. In these cases it is easier for students to connect with life on the margins, where there is an acceptance of the behaviors the school cannot condone. Well-trained and experienced counselors welcome this challenge and are aggressive in vesting the margins of school life and initiating a dialogue with students, getting to know them, and using their persuasive skills to connect these students to a counseling process.

As Robert L. Sinclair and Ward J. Ghory[1] suggest, forward-looking school principals, counselors, teachers, and parents bend over backward to create positive ties for positive connections. Students who are becoming marginalized receive a good deal of attention. Understanding how and why students become marginalized becomes a basis for action.

Therefore, the work involved in understanding how and why students become marginalized involves counselors collecting data by fully participating in the daily lives of marginalized students, whether it be in the counseling office, the classroom, the hallways, the cafeteria, before- and after-school activities, or home and community life—that is, going where the action is and understanding how these students interact in their world, hearing their language and learning firsthand what is going on in their lives.

Through this investigative process, counselors develop a more adequate picture of the issues preventing marginalized students from becoming achievers, and as a result of this they are able to develop an intervention plan that fits each student. Students respond to help when the message seems to fit them and their needs and is delivered by a counselor who knows them well and has established a degree of credibility, not a counselor who is office bound and only sees a student for scheduling, disciplining, and subtle warnings to shape up or be gone.

Sinclair and Ghory remind us that it is sobering to realize that any student is at risk of becoming at least temporarily disconnected from full and productive involvement in classrooms and school. They can be quickly knocked out of a pattern of productivity and go unnoticed in school for long periods. Unfortunately, these problems do not go away. They fester and can reach a boiling point in the late teen years. As a result of a lack of intervention, problems over time can become more complicated and serious. It is important for the "go to" personal counselors in the school to identify problematic students early and intervene. Time is not always a healer.

In this role, the counselor not only is an aggressive helper willing to seek out marginal students in their own haunts and comfort zones but also serves as a sort of investigative reporter who asks the following questions to himself about a student in need of help:

- What gives here? Why is this student unable and/or uninterested in achieving?
- What habits has he developed that are preventing his return to the mainstream of school life?
- What kind of interventions might help this student?

As these questions begin to be answered, the counselor's next step is to document this data for himself as well as for the building principal at the once-a-week principal-counselors meeting. In this way the story of the student in question becomes known to the principal, and the student is no longer simply a number identified only as a member of the at-risk group but is a real kid worth paying attention to and helping. Counseling marginalized students is a two-way process. For the counselor it's finding the right tone, the right style, the right time to connect with a student and sell her that the counselors have something of value to offer—demonstrating that he cares and offers support, comfort, trust, and, when needed, helpful confrontation.

For the student it means the opportunity to find a caring adult who knows something about her world and who might be able to help. It means finding a safe place, a cocoon, in which she can tell her story no matter how difficult this story may be, and she may somehow begin to have some aspirations, hopes, and excitement about turning her life around.

The settings for this kind of help can often go on outside the counselor's office with lunch in the cafeteria, walks around the school track, and even playing basketball in the gym. Troubled students usually avoid the office in their school. For them being summoned to an office, even a counselor's office, sends the message that they are in trouble. A veteran high school personal counselor told me that he often held counseling sessions in the back of the school where the smokers hung out.

Troubled kids have their safe places and counselors need to know where they are and use them. Help can go on in many places. It usually works best where students are comfortable. As such, personal counselors need to pay attention to their own office environment and make them welcoming settings, not just an office that is designed to "do business" and then get them out.

Personal counselors are different from counselors who interact with students around clerical tasks such as class scheduling, testing, etc. The world of personal counselors is all about finding meaning in encounters and situations with students, asking such questions as: What is this student's school and home life like? What goes on for him in school and at home? Is he a loner or connected to some group in school or the community? How does he see himself?

Does he have dreams, hopes, and aspirations? What has gone wrong in his life to separate him from the mainstream of school life? In this role the counselor participates in the lives of students and tries to overcome their resistance by respecting the students' norms, values, conflicts, and pressures although they may be very different from the counselor's own life. Acceptance of the other is critical for the offer of help to be welcomed. As the counselor gains entrance into the real lives of students, he often finds this territory very unfamiliar to his own life.

The world that students inhabit may seem problematic and to some extent unnatural to the counselor. As he gets to know a student, he may find himself learning lessons he didn't foresee. Helping students from diverse backgrounds can unsettle even an experienced counselor. Counselors are warned in their training that they may become involved with students who have problems that can unnerve them, make them feel anxious, and make them want to flee. Counselors who choose the quasi-administrative role often do so in order to avoid involvement in real-life stories of students who have seen many tragedies in their lives and seem lost, unable to find their place.

Skilled personal counselors are not immune to the pain of their students but are committed to staying with them as a helping process evolves—not an easy task or a role for the faint of heart. When one enters the real lives of students and observes them in their own environment and culture, one learns answers to questions that the students would not have had the sense to ask.

So when building principals; school psychologists; social workers; teachers; and community health, mental-health, and law enforcement professionals ask, "Does anyone know this kid, his background, family life?," the designated personal counselor can describe his interventions and what the school is doing to help him as well as his family members, some of whom may attend other schools in the district. In chronicling this student's story, the counselor is also prepared to describe outreach to these family members by referring them to the following possible sources of help:

- community health and mental-health agencies;
- social-service agencies;
- GED diploma and alternative high school graduation programs;
- food banks in the neighborhood;
- church outreach services;
- homeless shelters; and
- county child-abuse services.

This will provide pertinent information needed by the school and identify many open doors for help for the student as well as their families. In this role, the personal counselor becomes the expert in understanding the world that students inhabit in a large, complex high school and how they are either connected in a positive way to "their" school or at the margins of school life without any positive connections to a school in which they feel they have no place or connection. In his meetings with fellow counselors, teachers, and principals, he is then able to communicate the feelings that students have about "their" school and their relationship with peers, staff, and administration.

And he understands that his experience as an observer and chronicler of student behavior is always in flux, changing, as are the lives, values, and culture of students. Therefore, one of his critical skills is curiosity of just "What gives?" for students in his school and how parents, staff, and the administration react to student behaviors. This role requires that he insert himself into the lives of students and spend time where students hang out in both their school and their community.

In this process he seeks out caring adults in the school and community who offer an open door of help to students, areas of comfort that provide support for students trying to navigate through the ups and downs of teen life. These caring adults such as angel teachers, suspension-room teachers, eve-

ning recreational professionals, community health and mental-health workers, police, etc., all get enlisted in sharing their views of student life in the
school and community.

They are the "go to" adults that kids in need seek out and are the gate-
keepers of information about the kinds of problem students are having, what
interventions work to help them, and how the school can better serve them.
The personal counselor then is both a student and a learner in fitting together
what goes on in the personal, home, and social life of students who, as one
student reported, "Know the real deal, not the bullshit you hear at the PTA
meetings and workshops."

Trust is an important aspect of the personal counselor's role. He is not
gathering data to write a book or make a name for himself as an expert. He is
going to the source to better understand the students he has been trusted to
help, their lives, the adults they value, and those adults they stay away from.
This is not an easy role. Teenagers usually don't like adults, especially
school-related ones, hanging out where they hang. It takes skill to enter their
world as a person, not a professional, and be allowed to participate, listen,
and observe their interactions.

One has to be a "go to" person in their eyes who won't try to "teach"
them, "shape" them up, "counsel" them, be their "buddy," or pretend to be a
parent type who is "only looking out for their own good and simply wants to
correct them of their evil ways before it's too late." It is a tricky journey and
not every student group, particularly those at the margins, are going to quickly embrace the arrival of a personal counselor at their door. Trust takes time
and one has to put in the time, pay one's dues, to gain participation and, as
important, continue developing that trusting relationship, not letting it turn
sour.

Of course, that's true of any strong relationship. It needs to be nurtured.
Personal counselors understand that many of the troubled teens they encounter have had very negative experiences with their parents and other adults.
They are rightfully suspicious of do-gooders who they sense are out to "help"
them change their ways.

This kind of outreach takes time, time in selling their skills in a quiet way
to students who at first may resist their overtures and balk at any relationship
with a "counselor-type" person. Many troubled students have not experienced a positive relationship with counselors. Their welcome mat is not out.
In most cases, personal counselors have to enter the lion's den of student
lives many times before students are convinced that they are actually interested in learning about their lives. Resistance goes with the helping territory.
It's not easy, but if it works, the reward of knowing students well is priceless.

However, it is a role many counselors choose to avoid because of the time
required to deliver quality help and the lack of control they encounter when
entering the student's world. They are there as visitors on a trial basis, not as

professionals who are in charge and call the shots. It's not an easy role for counselors who have led their professional lives "being in charge and calling the shots" for students.

One of the basic questions that arise for personal counselors when they attempt to participate in a more meaningful way with their students is, "What side are you on?" Usually troubled teens have had confrontation with school authorities and have been suspended, done time in detention, been rated in the top quarter of the principal's at-risk kids list, and labeled as "trouble" and "watch out for this kid" by teachers. So it comes as no surprise that personal counselors are going to take some heat from students who have taken a lot of heat themselves.

It's a tricky role in which the counselor says he is here for himself because he wants to know and understand his students better, a statement that suggests that he is not responsible for what has happened to them in their school life nor is he in their world to blame others. He is in their world for himself. That's it. He is not a messenger sent by the school authorities to invade their space and spy on them. Rather he is there to hear their message so he can use their experience and information/data to help improve their school experience and increase the number of open doors for help that they and their peers may need someday, if not now.

This is not the kind of dialogue that usually goes on in the office of most counselors whose role has been focused on quasi-administrative duties. This kind of dialogue only goes on in counseling offices and settings in which students feel safe and welcomed, settings in which there is openness, respect, and mutuality between the counselor and students, settings that encourage a face-to-face exchange in which both students and counselors want to know more about each other's lives and what their dreams, hopes, and aspirations are—and for the counselors how they overcame the roadblock in their lives to become a student advocate, and for the students what the roadblocks are that they are facing now.

There should be an exchange in which the students can see the counselor as a human being and learn how he found the path to success that worked for him and who were the people in his life that told him, "You can," rather than, "You can't." Knowing the personal side of a counselor and learning about his way out of trouble often helps troubled students to begin to say, "I can," rather than, "I can't," or, "Don't even try."

This kind of counseling model is "getting to know each other" counseling. It's diametrically opposite the kind of counseling model called guidance, in which students visit the counselor for information on such topics as scheduling for classes, postsecondary education, financial aid, career information, and, in some schools, discipline infractions such as bullying, poor attendance, and low grades and failures. This is largely a role in which the counselor provides information and consequences.

This is a good fit for counselors who are skilled and interested in quasi-administrative tasks rather than offering personal counseling around personal, emotional, and well-being issues. These quasi-administrative counselors are a needed service for students and no doubt better in this role than a personal counseling role that they are not interested in nor suited for.

The personal counselor role, then, is very different. It is a role in which the counselor puts himself into the shoes of students in an attempt to experience events the way they experience them. And it also has a corresponding role for students who learn to put themselves in the shoes of the counselor when he was a teenager in an attempt to experience events in the way he experienced them, an exchange in which both the counselor and the student get to know each other well and learn the important lessons each of them have to offer the other.

In this counseling role the counselor and the student each become "teachers" and use their own life experience to understand, inform, and instruct each other. This counseling process doesn't always work smoothly but it is a process that every personal counselor should work hard to achieve. This process has great rewards for both the counselor and the students in helping make the school "their" school.

However, the personal counselor also needs to understand that he works in a highly politicized school world and needs to keep one foot in the world of students and the other in the world of colleagues, fellow counselors, teachers, and administrators. He needs to know well not only his student but also the educators he closely works with. He needs to be out of his office and seek out where students hang out and do the same with staff. The personal counselor can only succeed if he is committed to being out and about in the hallways, faculty rooms, staff dining area, and staff social events.

He needs to be seen as a trusted advocate not only for students but for staff as well, willing to listen to their concerns and intervene to help them out when the going gets tough with some students, colleagues, or out-of-school problems that are having a negative impact on their work performance. He straddles both the world of students and that of staff seeking common ground to bring the two worlds closer together as allies, not enemies.

This is a political process that requires ongoing close contact with both worlds. His success depends on being seen as not solely tied to the world of his students nor to the world of his colleagues so critics can raise the question, "Which side are you on?" He is a messenger for both sides with the goal of improving "their school."

This message has to honestly represent his observations, assessments, and professional impression of what goes on in the lives of his students and the best solutions available to improve their academic achievement as well as their social, emotional, and physical well-being. And this honest assessment needs to speak to the issue that some of the students' problems cited by education critics outside the school setting are not easily solved in our large high schools, as described in chapter 6.

NOTE

1. Robert L. Sinclair and Ward J. Ghory, "Last Thing First: Realizing Equity by Improving Conditions for Marginal Students," in *Access to Knowledge: An Agenda for the Nation's Schools*, ed. John Goodlad and Pamela Keating (New York: College Entrance Examination Board, 1990).

Chapter Six

The Role of the Personal Counselor as Adviser to the Principal

The major role of the personal counselor as advisor to his principal is to identify the kinds of interventions needed to help students achieve, be well, and have hopes, goals, and aspirations for their future. However, the personal counselor has another important role in pointing out to his principal the difficulty in solving student problems cited by educational critics who may have little awareness of what constitutes student life, values, culture, and behaviors in our large high school.

High schools are tough, are chaotic, and, at times, seem out of control from some critics who envision the school as a "peaceable kingdom" in which every student can be taught to like, respect, and value each other—where no bullying, fights, confrontation, and name-calling go on and students walk the hallways almost as if they had died and gone to heaven, where all is calm, low-key, and just a wonderful place to be. High schools in the real world are not like that or even close.

High school students make noise, a lot of it, act out, call each other names, cause fights, make fun of each other, and view the idea of a "peaceable kingdom" as a vision where students are anesthetized to keep quiet, be nice, not cause trouble, and be obedient. That's not the world high school students know, and thank god for that.

The personal counselor serving as a trusted advisor to the principal needs to help him sort out the difference between these two different worlds: one, the normal everyday behaviors of his students, and the other, the behaviors critics want for students. Many of these critics are raising their voices for principals to do more to radically change student behavior they view as out of control. Their favorite issues are bullying and sexual harassment by students. The personal counselor's role is to help his principal sort out just what constitutes bullying and sexual harassment versus what is simply the normal give and take among students. And it's also important to consider how the principal and the personal counselor act to educate critics that high schools will never be the peaceful kingdoms they dream about and envision.

While there are bullies and sexual harassers that need to be dealt with, the vast majority of student-to-student interactions are part of the culture of schools and adolescent life in which students need to learn how to survive in their often hostile, give-and-take world. These are tough calls for school administrators who are faced with juggling a fine line between what many high school students view "as normal," albeit hostile, verbal exchanges and what some students view as sexual harassment and bullying.

The role of administrators in helping teens with problems is never easy. They need help and support from many members of the community including personal counselors; teachers; coaches; students; support staff; parents; and community health, law, and social-service programs in order to provide many open doors for help. They can't get this job done on their own. There are too many students with problems and needs to be met arriving at the schoolhouse door each day.

But even when the helping resources of both the school and community are giving 100 percent, there are some societal-based problems that can present a great challenge—problems that outside experts and school reformers say high school principals are not giving a high priority to, or worse, are ignoring. Bullying and sexual harassment lead the list. Here's an example of the complex problems school leaders are facing.

According to *New York Times* reporter Jenny Anderson,[1] a national study by the National Association of University Women found widespread sexual harassment of students in grades 7 to 12. Nearly half of seventh- and twelfth-graders experienced sexual harassment in the last school year, with 87 percent of those who had been harassed reporting negative effects such as absenteeism, poor sleep, and stomach aches. Catherine Hill, the director of research at the association said, "It's pervasive, and almost a normal part of the school day." Holly Kearl, an author of the study, said, "Bullying is getting a lot of attention. We don't want schools to forget about sexual harassment and not talk about it."

What's missing from this and many reports about sexual harassment and bullying in our secondary schools is that these schools are turbulent, hostile, and highly sexualized. They are settings with large student populations, some housing over three thousand students. They're not places designed to help students form close personal relationships, be affirmed, be given recognition, and be given acceptance. Many of our secondary schools are survival courses for students and are tough places for teens who are not skilled to stand their ground. They are at-risk because they lack the skills to ward off bullies and harassers who can easily spot their vulnerabilities.

Teens who are unable to defend themselves then are raw meat in the hostile school culture. Yes, there are caring administrators, counselors, teachers, coaches, and support staff who daily try to protect at-risk kids. However, in some schools the ongoing, daily demands of student troubles and conflict overwhelm them, particularly in urban communities.

While the school public relations announcements may state there is zero tolerance for sexual harassment and bullying, this proclamation has no real chance of succeeding. Our large secondary schools are not peaceable kingdoms and never will be, nor will every student be a peacemaker. Suggesting these schools can be reorganized to be peaceable kingdoms is a wish, a prayer, a hope, but a denial of what these schools are really like.

Many of these schools were built and organized in the 1950s for a far different world and student/parent population; in today's world schools are facing many more complex student problems, bullying and sexual harassment being two of many. The student culture in today's schools is highly confrontational.

When Ms. Hill says, "It's pervasive, and almost a natural part of school life," she is right. But she has a false perception of secondary schools if she believes this is a school culture that is completely out of control and demands fixing. Her comment misses the point that the student culture of secondary schools is about surviving the daily battles and conflicts between individual students and peer groups. And it's a culture in which a major focus of student life and communication is on sex. It is a time of sexual awakening and much of the conversations between students are sexually laden, provocative, and filled with wanted or unwanted sexual advances with words such as "you're so hot."

It's a culture in which there is a fine line between what is "normal," sometimes-hostile, sometimes-sexual verbal exchanges between students and exchanges that can be labeled as sexual harassment and bullying. We live in tough times and many teens come to school angry with their world and the growing lack of opportunity for themselves and family members. And we live in a world that is highly sexual and many teens come to school to explore their sexuality and that exploration often begins with trial and error.

What may be seen by outside experts and educational reformers as inappropriate sexual advances are often seen by students as simply flirtations and a "normal" part of this process of connecting and "checking each other out." For many students, making inappropriate, irreverent, and colorful comments are a deeply ingrained and a harmless part of the school culture. Most students are not weak, defenseless, and are able to deal with these sometimes-uncomfortable and hostile situations. It's school life as they know it.

However, there are students who arrive at school as tender creatures, unable to deal with these uncomfortable and hostile conversations. They should be our concern, and we should help them learn the necessary skills and toughness now required to survive in a culture in which being nice and turning the other cheek can be risky.

It is, as Ms. Hill described, "an almost a normal part of the school day." In these verbal exchanges some students will use hostile verbal comments to spar with peers. For example, casually using words such as *slut, dick, homo, whore, piece of ass, built for speed, gay, so hot, shit, ugly, well built, bitch,* and *horny*—words that may appear as sexual harassment or bullying, but are in reality a normal part of the everyday language used by teens to connect or disconnect from each other.

For students, it's all about developing communication skills that help them to be adept at dealing with uncomfortable and hostile encounters because that's what secondary school life is all about. Yes, hostile and sexual communications, but not exchanges that cross the line into sexual harassment or bullying.

In the school culture of who survives and who becomes a victim, negative labels and words are the centerpiece of school life. For many outsiders such as school reformers and sexual harassment/bullying experts, it is not a fair, peaceful, kind, accepting, or gentle use of dialogue. They envision a school world in which students are quiet, civilized, helpful, and kind to each other, never rude or hostile, and sexually laden conversations are absent.

However, for many students it's "their" language and way of communicating. Inappropriate comments are championed. It's the law of the jungle in the school culture. Be prepared to battle and defend yourself or be victimized.

As adults the behaviors we may want for students are often not the behaviors students want for themselves. In today's school world there is great pressure from concerned educators and parents to get school leaders to create a culture absent of hostility and sexual overtones. This is a difficult situation for administrators, who must walk a fine line between hearing critics who are calling for zero tolerance for sexual harassment and bullying and standing up for a school culture in which "normal" verbal exchanges between students are part of their world and do not cross the line into sexual harassment and bullying.

Administrators who have the responsibility for making the "right" judgment call in sexual harassment and bullying cases are presented with a fine, gray line to navigate. These administrators have enough on their hands without the pressure to make their school environment peaceable kingdoms, absent of hostility. Many of their schools are overcrowded with outdated facilities, serving diverse student groups who are often in conflict with each other, and staff working in an environment in which student problems are always on the increase.

There is no respite for them and few rewards. They're in a war that seems to never end. Adding proposals to make their schools peaceable kingdoms seems so far removed from the reality they face each day that it borders on the absurd. However, this does not mean that bullying and sexual harassment doesn't exist in our large secondary schools. Educative and preventative measures need to be in place to protect students who may be victimized.

Researcher Catherine Hill and author Holly Kearl are right when they say, "Bullying is getting a lot of attention, we don't want schools to forget about sexual harassment and not talk about it." Action is required when clear cases of bullying and sexual harassment arise. And the personal counselor is well positioned to advise his principal on how to implement preventative measures.

For example, the personal counselor understands that parents who raise their children to be nice, quiet, peace loving, and safe; to avoid conflict; to like everyone; and to find some good in everyone are not doing them a favor. In fact, their kindness and good intentions to be good parents may be actually helping make their children at risk once they reach secondary school. These children are being raised without the skills to face conflict when it comes their way, conflict that will surely visit them when they enter middle school, junior high, and high school.

These students often have an aura of innocence about them and signal to more aggressive peers that they are raw meat, unable to defend themselves. Here is an example of how the personal counselor enters the world of his principal, parents, and students. It's a three-step educative and intervention process to help resolve the politicized issues that surround bullying and sexual harassment cases.

Step 1 provides intervention for students who have been identified as ongoing aggressive bullies and sexual harassers. This process is two-fold. The principal strongly advises them and their parents that they have a serious problem and consequences are in store such as suspensions. Action will be taken. The personal counselor provides counseling intervention for them to learn to be less aggressive, confrontational, and accepting of more-vulnerable peers.

Step 2 provides intervention for students who appear to be the target of hostile behavior by peers. Here the personal counselor offers the necessary training for vulnerable students on how to confront aggressive peers and seek help when they find themselves becoming victims.

Step 3 involves the personal counselor engaging parents in a series of forums to educate parents about their responsibility in raising children who are resilient, can stand their ground, and know how to deter bullies and sexual harassers. In this role he takes the lead in educating parents about the real student's life that goes on in their high school, not the critic's dream of school as a peaceable kingdom, and their role in preparing their children for this often-turbulent scene.

In these educative forums the personal counselor message is teach your children the skills they will need "in their" life—not the life you are planning for them, as this will inadvertently make them victims. Schools can do their best to offer support for students who are raised in families like this by providing many open doors for help: support groups, teacher advisors, individual counseling, etc. But in the end, what is needed is an increased effort by parents to raise resilient children who can stand on their own. To argue that school leaders can and should do more to make their schools peaceable kingdoms and their students peacemakers is an unrealistic goal in today's complex school world with its many demands.

The personal counselor role in preventing bullying is to reach out to parents to get them on board a training program that emphasizes preparing their children to expect bullying and providing them with the skills to confront bullies and providing them with the resources to seek help when needed—help that includes their role as caring parents and intervention specialists in the school such as the personal counselor. In this role, parents are trained on how to speak to their children about the skills they need in order to prevent being a victim but also the importance of acting quickly to get help if the bullying persists.

To make this intervention system work, the personal counselor organizes a schoolwide network of allies, such as the school administrators, school nurse, teachers, students, support staff, custodians, and bus drivers, who are prepared and expected to intervene when they observe a student in trouble, creating a circle of wellness that can respond to students when trouble visits them and they see no way out. Bad things do happen to good kids. And bad things that happen to good kids have a much greater chance of happening in schools that lack a personal counselor for intervention for students and training for staff and parents.

For example, reporter Carol Lloyd describes in her article "One R-Rated Movie You Might Want Your Child to See"[2] the cases of the five children being bullied as portrayed in the documentary *Bully*. it appears that none of the above intervention and training programs were in place, or even considered. It seems that almost everyone in the school and community either observed or knew about these troubled kids who were at the margins of school and community life with no help on the way.

The father of one victim, Tyler Long, a seventeen-year-old student from Georgia, said he was shoved into a wall locker, beat up on the school bus, told he was worthless, and told to go hang himself. No one in the school seems to have intervened and provided an open door for help. He was on his own, and in the end he hung himself. With no doors of help open and seemingly too overwrought to continue the battle, he chose death by hanging.

Another victim, Ja'Meya Jackson, a fourteen-year-old African American middle school student from Mississippi with good grades and a quiet demeanor, was labeled as a Goody Two Shoes. One day she snapped and brought her mother's loaded gun onto the school bus and waved the butt around to show she wasn't taking it anymore. No one was hurt, but as the documentary suggests, she was pushed to the brink by the constant ridicule she experienced day by day because she was a high-achieving student and was quiet. Seemingly unable to protect herself or ask for help before she "snapped," Ja'Meya was charged with forty-five felony counts.

It appears the school hallways and school buses are dangerous territory; the documentary calls them "war zones," with no protection for students who are defenseless, not prepared to ward off bullies or ask for help before it is too late. These are often students who find themselves at the margins of school and community life, isolated and oppressed, such as a new, obese, gay, strange, or too-bright student—students who are loners, not part of the crowd, and have been taught by many life experiences to fly under the radar, be invisible, or otherwise trouble will find them.

The question is why wasn't there intervention when the abuse was so rampant? It seemed everyone looked the other way—administrators, counselors, teachers, students, bus drivers—until the students involved "snapped" and lives were lost or changed for the worse. As the documentary suggests, the adults failed again and again to intervene. Or when they intervened, their intervention was only added to the abuse the child was experiencing because they lacked the skills, compassion, and desire to stop the abuse. For example, in one scene a father chides his son for being bullied, inquiring if he "actually liked it."

In another scene a teacher pressures a bullied boy to shake hands with his clearly unrepentant tormentor. When the bullied child refuses, the teacher suggests it's his fault for not being friendly—not the kind of parent or teacher an abused student should seek out when trouble visits them. The school's role is to educate students about whom they can turn to when things get out of control in their school or home life, and parents need to be trained how to come to the aid of their children when the bottom is falling out in their lives.

No intervention system or parent-training program is perfect, but those in leadership positions in the schools need to make the necessary effort, which must be ongoing, to make certain other Tylers and Ja'Meyas meet a better fate. Any school lacking highly skilled and aggressive intervention specialists and trainers for staff, students, parents, and community helping resources is risking their students to abuse such as bullying.

For example, the documentary points out how the principals and school board members involved spin their "kids will be kids" PR campaigns, exonerating themselves of responsibility. In one scene a principal assures parents whose sons have been repeatedly assaulted and whose heads have been pressed beneath a bus seat by saying, "I've been on that bus and those kids are as good as gold." Bad things happen to good kids when those charged with their safekeeping—bus drivers, hall monitors, teachers, or school princi-pals—look the other way or suggest that all is well when it isn't. *Bully* suggests that the education professionals involved may have been clueless, "but they meant no harm."

But no skilled educators can come away from this documentary saying, "No harm was done." Harm was done to defenseless kids because the schools involved had no clear pathways to help troubled kids, whether they are on a bus, in a hallway, or abused at home by a callous parent who challenges his son's masculinity, inability to fight back, and suggests that "he likes to be bullied."

The message for students in schools without skilled intervention special-ists such as a personal counselor is that they are fair game for the same kind of abuse and when it happens it's up to them to defend themselves and there is no one else in their corner. Some students are lucky, as they have been prepared by their parents for such abuse and have the skills to confront such abuse. But there are students like Tyler and Ja'Meya, the bright girl with the quiet demeanor, who lack the necessary skills, support, and resources to fight back and save themselves before it's too late. These quiet, defenseless teens who are unable to fight back are the ones that can be saved by skilled personal counselors and their team of allies. They are not hard to spot or help. They are waiting.

And often it is the openly gay kid who receives the most physical and emotional blows. These students often get risky advice from gay and lesbian organizations to "come out" and announce to the entire school and commu-nity they are gay. As a result what often happens is these students immediate-ly become targets for harassment from some groups in the school and com-munity who are against homosexuality. And that harassment can be mean-spirited and push vulnerable students to the brink, sometimes resulting in them committing suicide to escape the brutality they are experiencing.

It may be a safer course for gay and lesbian students to refrain from public announcements and behaviors concerning their sexuality and avoid becoming cheerleaders for gay and lesbian organizations who fail to either consider the dangers they are exposing these students to in their schools and community or, worse, who knowingly use these students as poster children for their movement and put them at great risk. A better course may be for students to embrace their sexuality quietly and not become targets.

The case of fourteen-year-old Kenneth Weishuhn Jr. is an example of what can go wrong when a teen publicly announces he has "come out" in a school where there are no personal counselors to counsel and advise him and no intervention system, no safety wall, to protect him. As Associated Press[3] reports, Kenneth was a freshman at South O'Brien High School in Paullina, Iowa. He killed himself in April, 2012, in what police describe as a "self-inflicted injury." Here are the highlights as reported by the Associated Press:

- His mother, Jamie Chambers, knew he was harassed but said she and the rest of the family didn't realize the extent of the bullying. She said her son dismissed her concerns over the bullying and hid his pain behind a smile. She said when Kenneth came out in early spring of 2012 to his family and friends he quickly became the target of threatening cell phone calls, voice-mails, and online comments on his Facebook page, including death threats.
- His sister Kayla, a sophomore in the school, said her brother's life took a turn for the worse when he came out. She said, "He was pretty popular, he had lots of friends, but once they found out he was gay, a lot of them turned on him." Kayla said, "I was really mad because those guys were supposed to be my friends and they were making fun of my brother. I tried to stick up for him a couple of times, but I guess it wasn't enough."
- Dan Moore, the superintendent of the South O'Brien Community School District, said administrators knew of only one incident regarding Kenneth and he believed they dealt with it well. He said, "Obviously we had no idea that we'd have an end result like this, or what was going on outside of here."
- Kenneth's mother said the school administrators didn't do enough to protect her son and they never reached out to her about the harassment her son was facing.
- Kenneth told his mom, "Mom, you don't know how it feels to be hated."
- The *Sioux City Journal*[4] devoted a front-page story to Kenneth's death and in their editorial reported, "The warnings were everywhere."

As the editorial board of the *Sioux City Journal* suggests, the warning signs were everywhere. It appears the red lights of danger were flashing throughout the school and community. But it seems the school had no "go to" person to observe, monitor, and intervene to help Kenneth before it was too late. There are many students like Tyler Long, Je'Meya Jackson, and Kenneth Weishuhn Jr. waiting for our help.

The guidance and counseling model I am proposing creates the opportunity for each of the roles, the quasi-administrative counselor and the personal counselor, to play an important role in helping "their" principal, students, and parents to be successful. Principals need the expert intervention of both the quasi-administrative counselors and the personal counselors working in tandem to help reduce student failures, discipline problems, suspensions, and dropouts and increase academic success and postsecondary rates.

These two counseling roles can come to the aid of each other and need each other. The quasi-administrative counselors need the expertise of personal counselors to help troubled students resolve their problems and become successful academic students. The personal counselors need the expertise of quasi-administrative counselors to help channel their students into higher education and career opportunities. They are a team with team players who respect each other's roles and have each other's backs. In today's school world, where turf is heavily guarded and the old ways of doing business dominate, this model may only exists as a blueprint and a dream, but it is a very doable dream.

Here is an example. When a quasi-administrative counselor is facing resistance in trying to guide a troubled student into attending school more often and staying out of conflict, he can ask the personal counselor to help out. Conversely, when the personal counselor makes a breakthrough with a troubled student who now wants to succeed in school and get into a "good" college, he can ask his colleague who is well versed in college admissions to lend a hand. In this process, they work hand in hand doing what they both do best, helping students in their own way.

This model, based on equal value for both the personal and quasi-administrative counselors in the guidance and counseling organization, would help bring clarity of purpose to counselors' day-by-day responsibilities and the reality they are facing as professionals in their schools. As the report "Counseling at the Crossroads"[5] reveals, many counselors are frustrated with their profession, with their role in the schools, and with themselves as professionals. The present model is an incubator that generates frustration and needs to be changed. Here are some of the key complaints by counselors cited in the report:

- They feel their mission is unclear and needs to be more clearly defined.
- They say they are involved in a "profession in search of an identity," and are disenchanted with their profession and the schools in which they work, and left out of the education-reform movement.
- They see a disturbing gap between what the mission of their professions should be and the reality they are facing as professionals in schools.
- They feel their role as counselors is frequently murky with poorly defined goals, lacking clarity of purpose both in their day-to-day responsibilities and as a part of the broader education system that may place them with one foot inside the traditional education system and the other foot in a network of mental- and social-support services that is not uniformly tied to the rest of the education system.
- They feel they are caught between cross currents asking them to play very different roles, thus limiting their effectiveness.

Here is a more in-depth assessment of some of the major highlights and recommendations of the "Counseling at the Crossroads" report.

School counselors are highly valuable professionals in the education system, but they are also among the least strategically deployed. This is a national loss, especially given the fact that school counselors are uniquely positioned, in ways that many educators are not, to have a complete picture of the dreams, hopes, life circumstances, challenges, and needs of their students. Counselors have both a holistic view of the students in their schools and the opportunity to provide targeted supports to keep these students on track for success, year after year.

For the past century, counselors have been hard at work performing many roles in their schools, from guiding student decision-making, helping students to address personal problems, and working with parents, to administering tests, teaching, and filling other gaps unrelated to counseling. Counselors' roles have been as diverse as the students they serve, often resulting in an unclear mission, a lack of accountability for student success, and having school counseling seen as a "profession in search of identity." Consequently, even though there are nearly as many school counselors as administrators across America, counselors have been largely left out of the education-reform movement.

To understand the perspectives of counselors, the College Board Advocacy & Policy Center, Civic Enterprises, and Peter D. Hart Research Associates collaborated to survey 5,308 middle and high school counselors, which is the largest and broadest national survey of these education professionals to date. We sought insight into how they view their roles and missions and spend their days, as we believe they might be more strategically deployed to better serve students.

We also were interested in their perspectives on measures of accountability and education policies and practices that could strengthen their roles and the systems in which they work. We hoped to learn what challenges they face and what solutions might be found to better leverage the extraordinary resource that school counselors represent.

We are at a crossroads in American education in defining the role our nation's school counselors will play to help improve student achievement. America is fast losing its place in the world in the highest levels of educational attainment. The costs to students, communities, the economy, and our nation merit an urgent national response, one that included our counselors.

At a time when school district dollars are more constrained than ever, and when one in four public school students fails to graduate on time, now is the time to be highly strategic with these precious educational resources. We share the perspective of school counselors to better understand how the school counselor, a critical component of the education sector and an underutilized tool in education reform, can be better leveraged to promote student achievement and ensure that more students graduate from high school ready for college and their careers.

This survey of more than 5,300 middle school and high school counselors reveals deep concerns within the profession and sheds light on opportunities to better utilize these valuable leaders in America's schools. The frustrations and hopes of school counselors reflect the central message of this report: school counseling as a profession is at a crossroads.

Despite the aspirations of counselors to effectively help students succeed in school and fulfill their dreams, the mission and roles of counselors in the education system must be more clearly defined; schools must create measures of accountability to track their effectiveness; and policymakers and key stakeholders must integrate counselors into reform efforts to maximize their impact in schools across America.

School counselors believe their mission should be to prepare children for high school graduation, college, and careers, and they report that they are ready to lead in the effort to dramatically accelerate student achievement in school careers and life. Counselors, on average, have high expectations for themselves, their students, their schools, and the education system, but reality falls far short of their hopes. Our survey shows that counselors are, in large part, disenchanted with both the reality of their profession and the schools in which they work.

In fact, the majority of counselors are calling for changes in the educational system. Counselors are also largely enthusiastic about supporting college- and career-readiness initiatives, but here again, do not think they have the support and resources to successfully promote their students' postsecondary achievement. Altogether, the majority of counselors report a broken system that does not align with their aspirations for their students. They call for changes to the system, want to help lead these reform efforts in their schools, and ask for more support to fulfill their mission.

Moving from a macro education systems discussion to a school-based one, counselors report a similarly disturbing gap between what the mission of their profession should be and the reality they are facing as professionals in schools. The two highest-rated ideal missions for counselors are "to be advocates for all students within the school system" and "to inspire students to reach their full potential and achieve their goals" (these were both rated a nine or ten on a ten-point scale by 92 percent of counselors).

In an ideal context three additional missions rank just below serving as advocates and inspiring students: "addressing student problems so students stay in school through graduation" (85 percent rate this a nine or ten on a ten-point scale); "ensuring students earn a diploma and are ready to succeed in college and careers" (84 percent); and "helping students mature and develop the interpersonal skills they will need to succeed in the adult world" (83 percent).

As with the mission for the education system, counselors report major gaps between what they would ideally like to see and what they are experiencing in schools. The largest gap is seen for the mission of helping students mature and develop skills for the real world, of which 83 percent of counselors say it closely fits their view of the ideal mission, but just 33 percent say it closely fits their mission in reality, a gap of 50 points. There also is a large gap of 43 points for the mission of inspiring students to reach their full potential and achieve their goals, where 92 percent of counselors say it closely fits their view of the ideal mission, but just 49 percent say it closely fits their mission in reality.

The role of the counselors is frequently murky, with poorly defined goals that may place them with one foot inside the traditional education system and the other foot in a network of mental- and social-support services that is not uniformly tied to the rest of the education system. Counselors report lacking clarity of purpose both in their day-to-day responsibilities and as a part of the broader education system.

Despite the increased focus in the United States on academic success and postsecondary achievement, current state and federal laws pertaining to school counseling are limited; counselors have remained largely in the background of major school reform initiatives. In all, much of the confusion and poor deployment of school counselors across the education system seems to arise from what has been described as a "general lack of understanding by critical stakeholders about what school counselors do that impacts student outcomes."

This lack of role clarity may prevent counselors from maximizing their impact on the lives of children. School counselors are a vital part of the education system and play key roles in supporting students in holistic ways. These professionals, who are often former teachers themselves, are uniquely positioned to support student achievement, not just because of their specialized education, but because they have a more compete, year-to-date perception of every student they counsel, understanding their hopes and dreams

The "Counseling the Crossroads" report is hard-hitting and uses the words and observations of counselors to show their frustration with the way their work is now organized, highlighting their feelings that they are caught between crosscurrents asking them to play many different roles, thus limiting their effectiveness.

The good news is that if counselor leaders and administrators listen and hear the words in this report, they will be shown "the way." This report provides new organizational model and paradigm to follow, one that provides counselors with a mission and roles in which they can be successful and meet their mandate to be of help and service to students, parents, staff, and their principals.

The key piece to reorganizing guidance and counseling programs to meet the needs of students in today's complex world is providing alternatives for counselors being asked to play many different roles, thus limiting their effectiveness. Put simply, high school counselors cannot be expected to successfully accomplish all the different roles asked of them: college-prep counseling, scheduling students for classes, administering and supervising mandated testing programs, career and vocational counseling, and attendance and discipline counseling.

And on top of all these tasks, they are expected to offer personal counseling interventions, such as the ASCA recommendations for responsive service to address students' direct, immediate concerns and include counseling, consultation, and referral as well as system support, such as professional development, consultation, and collaboration with staff, administration, and community agencies.

Something has to give in this out-of-date model that counselors are saddled with. And the "Counseling at the Crossroads" report exposes clearly the confusion, poor deployment, and lack of role clarity that prevents counselors from maximizing their impact on the lives of children.

And, often, the result when personal counseling services are not available to help needy and marginalized students is that they are left to seek help on their own. And some find themselves preyed upon by messiah teachers, as described in *Innocent Denied: A Guide to Preventing Sexual Misconduct by Teachers and Coaches*,[6] who cross professional boundaries and entice these students into being close friends and even lovers.

Unfortunately, instead of resolving their troubles, these students end up more troubled and in trouble because they were blinded by the messiah teacher's real intent. The harsh truth is that many troubled teens in need of help are so desperate for an adult connection that they'll enter any door that seems safe and welcoming and miss the signs of danger present. They are looking for love in all the wrong places because their school lacks a safe open door for help, such as a personal counselor ready and set to help, danger-free and risk-free.

The messiah teacher's role in harming needy teenagers usually arises when the role of guidance counselors is murky or nonexistent when it comes to intervening to help troubled teens. As the "Counseling at the Crossroads" report suggests, the role of the counselor is frequently murky, with poorly defined goals that may place them with one foot inside the traditional education system and the other foot in a network of mental- and social-support services that is not uniformly tied to the rest of the education system and lacks a legitimate place in the school hierarchy.

It should come of no surprise that counselors report lacking clarity of purpose both in their day-to-day responsibilities and as a part of the broader education system. They are hearing two contradicting voices of "what they should be doing," and the one that often wins out is the one with the foot in the traditional education system in which their role as a quasi-administrator is focused on increasing the rates of student attendance, test scores, postsecondary education, class scheduling, and reducing student discipline rates. The role that loses out is the one with the other foot in a network of mental- and social-support services that are not uniformly tied to the rest of the education system. These are the responsive services and system support interventions recommended in the ASCA report.

The answer to how students can be privy to the guidance of counselors serving in the role of quasi-administrators with a foot in the traditional education system and personal counselors involved in mental and social support is clear: identifying and positioning skilled counselors in each area, thus bringing them together as one team whose components offer different but equally important services with both feet now in the same camp, partners doing what they each do best.

In this model everyone knows their job and is ready and set to help, not being asked to fulfill mandates that are beyond what they are capable of delivering, thus closing the gap and frustration between what the mission of their profession should be and the reality they are facing in their schools.

The plan of the high school principals described in the LinkedIn online chat in chapter 3—to reorganize their guidance staff—is a needed new counseling program model. That plan called for a reconfiguration of the counseling staff, assigning two counselors for attendance, two for scheduling, two for counseling, and one for college admissions. The response to this new paradigm was met with great resistance from the counselor involved as well as other counselors who assessed the plan as "ludicrous." In this model, the principal is focusing in on the specific "skills" of counselors on his staff and where they can be best placed for the guidance and counseling program to be effective. This kind of differentiated staffing model holds the key to the future success of the conquering professionals: each counselor doing what they do well as individuals and as team members and acting in total support of their principal, who needs a revamped counseling department in order to successfully lead his school through these complicated and turbulent times.

However, the resistance of counselors to a different model to organize their work from what they have known needs to be recognized and acknowledged in any change process. As stated in the LinkedIn exchanges, counselors will say the new model suggested by the principal is "ludicrous." And *ludicrous* is a tame word compared to the words of resistance that many counselors will use when real change is on the horizon.

Counselors may say they are frustrated and disenchanted and caught between cross currents asking them to play far too many different roles that limit their effectiveness but when presented with a new paradigm, model, they often say things like, "Nice idea, but not now; let's put it off until the current crisis situation calms down. We need more study and input to find out what other schools are doing. The scuttlebutt is there are very few schools using this model. There must be a reason! What we are doing now may have its problems but we've been doing it for years. Every job has its frustrations. Let's not through the baby out with the bath water."

However, as a Charles Duhigg suggests in his book, *The Power of Habit: Why We Do What We Do in Life and Business*,[7] changing the habits of workers in an organization can be done. Here are some observations from Duhigg's book that may be helpful to counselors, leaders, and principals to win over resisting counselors stuck in old habits:

- For a habit to stay changed, people must believe change is possible. And most often that belief only emerges with the help of a group.
- Habits cannot be eradicated; they must be replaced. To change a habit, you must find an alternative routine and your odds of success go up dramatically when you commit to changing as part of a group; belief is essential and it grows out of a communal experience.
- We know that change can happen. Alcoholics can stop drinking; smokers can quit puffing; perennial losers can become champions. We can stop biting nails and snacking at work, yelling at our kids, staying up all night, or worrying over small concerns. And as scientists have discovered, it's not just individual lives that can shift when habits are tended to. It's also companies, organizations, and communities.
- Small wins are part of how keystone habits create widespread change. Once a small win has been accomplished, focuses are set in motion that favor another small win. Small wins fuel transformative changes by leveraging tiny advances into patterns that convince people that bigger achievements are within range.
- If people are asked to do something that takes self-control, if they think they are doing it for personal reasons, and they are doing it to help someone else, it's much less taxing than if they feel they have no autonomy. If they feel they are just following orders, their willpower muscles get tired much faster. In companies and organizations, simply giving people a sense of agency, a feeling that they are in control, that they have genuine decision-making authority, can radically increase how much energy and focus they bring to their jobs.
- It may seem like most organizations make rational choices based on deliberate decision-making, but that's not really how companies operate at all. Instead, firms are guided by long-held organizational habits.
- Most economists are accustomed to treating companies as idyllic places where everyone is devoted to a common goal such as making as much money as possible. However, in the real world, that's not how things work at all. Companies aren't big happy families where everyone plays nice together. Rather, most workplaces are made up of fiefdoms where executives compete for power and credit, often in hidden skirmishes that make their own performance appear superior and their rivals' seem worse. Divisions compete for resources and sabotage each other to steal glory. Bosses

pit their subordinates against one another so that no one can mount a coup. Companies are not families; they're battlefields of civil war.

- Good leaders seize crisis to make organizational habits. For example, NASA administrators tried for years to improve the agency's safety habits but those efforts were unsuccessful until the space shuttle Challenger exploded in 1986. In the wake of this tragedy, the organization was able to overhaul how it enforced quality standards.
- A company with dysfunctional habits can't turn around simply because a leader orders it. Rather, wise executives seek out moments of crisis, or create the perception of crisis, and cultivate the sense that "something must change" until everyone is finally ready to overhaul the patterns they live with each day. You never let a crisis go to waste. Crisis provides the opportunity to do things you could not do before.
- Changing habits requires willpower. Willpower isn't just a skill. It's a muscle and it gets tired. If you want to do something that requires willpower, you have to conserve your willpower muscle. If you use it up on tedious tasks like filling out forms, all your strength will be gone.

Duhigg suggests that once you understand that habits can change, you have the freedom and responsibility to remake them. Once you understand that habits can be rebuilt, the power becomes easier to grasp, and the only option left is to get to work.

Real change in the way counseling services are organized calls for a change of old habits and the creation of a different vision. Counselors have to be sold on the "new" and why it will help them to be more effective. The process of "selling" counselors needs to begin with counselor leaders and principals building on the anger, frustration, and disenchantment of counselors with the present system and providing them ample time to vent and share their feelings of being trapped in a profession in search of an identity. This kind of process allows counselors the freedom to look closely at what is not working well and to be open to hearing alternatives to the way their work is organized.

Then, after the venting process is finished, follow it with the observation that the main reason that the counselor's role is frequently murky with poorly defined goals is that they are placed with one foot inside the traditional education system performing a quasi-administrative role and the other foot in a network of mental- and social-support services that is not uniformly tied to the rest of the school system. Their role historically has been divisive, placing them in two different camps with differing goals and priorities.

As a result, when counselors are asked to accomplish these differing goals, they can't. The present system won't allow it, as the demands of the traditional education system employing the quasi-administrative counselors as their go-to person always wins over personal counseling, which, in a two-part organizational system, is often relegated to a low priority or simply ignored because the quasi-administrative role as arranged in the now-outdated counselor delivery system yields data and gets credit and awards for raising postsecondary school rates, test scores, etc., while the personal counselor role receives little credit because there is little activity or data collection.

It's vacant territory existing in name only, orphaned, out of the spotlight, and until now never able to take its seat at the table. The selling of a new organization model to counselors begins with educating them that much of their confusion is due to their training in "counseling" in graduate school and the reality they are facing as counselors in their schools in which their priority is serving as a quasi-administrative counselor. This confusion can be erased by assigning some counselors to serve as quasi-administrators and others to serve as personal counselors, thus eliminating the murkiness that has placed them in two different camps but in reality only charging them to serve one camp.

Changing old habits of counselors and getting them aboard a new delivery system will require a strong sales campaign including the following components:

- the strong support of the building principal;
- a new awareness about how and why their current system is making them frustrated, disenchanted, and in crisis;
- challenging them as individuals and as a group to put their effort and willpower behind a new system;
- educating and training them to envision a role for themselves in this new scheme both as individuals and as team members;
- role-playing how the new roles of counselors serving as quasi-administrators and personal counselors would play out in the everyday operation of the guidance and counseling department;
- role-playing how weekly principal-counselor meetings would provide needed data and information about the counseling delivery system and system support;
- role-playing how the personal counseling role would play out in the everyday operation of the guidance and counseling department; and
- maintaining focus on small wins in which members of counseling teams observe, document, and chronicle examples of how they have helped student, parent, staff member, administrator, counselor colleague, etc.— "how to" data that can be shared at counselor team meetings, principal-counselor meetings, staff meetings, child study committee meetings, PTA meetings, and school-community forums, all venues that can be used to demonstrate how the counseling team comes to the aid of various members of the school community.

The next chapter will focus on how a principal, counselor, and school nurse sold the personal counseling model to counselors, teachers, parents, and students by demonstrating how an intervention with addicted students helped redirect the lives of marginal students headed toward dropping out.

NOTES

1. Jenny Anderson, "Widespread Sexual Harassment in Grades 7 to 12," *New York Times*, November 7, 2011, available online at www.nytimes.com/2011/11/07/education/widespread-sexual-harassment-in-grades-7-to-12-found-in-study.html?_r=0 (accessed March 21, 2013).

2. Carol Lloyd, "One R-Rated Movie You Might Want Your Child to See," *Great Schools*, www.greatschools.org/parenting/bullying/6317-bullying-school-movie.gs (accessed March 21, 2013).

3. Associated Press, "Mother of Gay Iowa Teen Blames Suicide on School, Online Bullying: Authorities Investigating," www.foxnews.com/us/2012/04/18/iowa-mom-blames-gay-teen-son-suicide-on-school (accessed April 23, 2012).

4. Associated Press, "Iowa Paper Devotes Front Page to Fighting Bullying," April 22, 2012, www.foxnews.com/us/2012/04/22/iowa-paper-devotes-front-page-to-fighting-bullying-596408376 (accessed March 21, 2013).

5. The College Board, "Counseling at the Crossroads," National Office of School Counseling Advocacy, 2011, pp. 4, 5, 12, 17, 21.

6. William L. Fibkins, *Innocent Denied: A Guide to Preventing Sexual Misconduct by Teachers and Coaches* (Lanham, MD: Rowman & Littlefield, 2006).

7. Charles Duhigg, *The Power of Habit: Why We Do What We Do in Life and Business* (New York: Random House, 2012), 92, 137, 139, 151, 162, 178.

Chapter Seven

Selling the Personal Counseling Role with a Successful Intervention Program

This chapter presents an example that can help members of the school community understand the *why* for the necessity of a personal counselor role in bringing back marginal students from the edge of dropping out, helping them become responsible and successful members of the school community. This example demonstrates the important leadership role of building principals in encouraging, supporting, and risking new approaches to help troubled students and parents—an extremely important role in readying our high school organizations to solve the problem of today's students and abandon the out-of-date 1950s intervention model.

What follows is a true story of how a group of addicted students were brought into the helping process and learned that they could develop skills and support to choose another lifestyle. And, in the process, become skilled at the helping process and committed to reaching out and helping their peers. An example of how students can come back from the margins of school life to take a central role as leaders in the helping process, becoming "somebodies" instead of "nobodies."

The key to engaging these students who were estranged from the school community was the deployment of a team composed of the school principal, the nurse, and a personal counselor who was a member of the school guidance staff with the job description of offering individual and group counseling to students; training teachers as advisors; counseling students in the school's alternative education program; training students, support staff, and parents as peer counselors; and offering intervention groups on health and wellness issues such as tobacco, smoking, drugs, alcohol, and eating disorders.

The personal counselor worked as a team member with other counselors who were happily assigned, in their words, to the quasi-administrative tasks of college admissions, testing, scheduling, and career counseling. They were not expected to do discipline counseling, which was provided by two assistant principals.

This new differentiated staffing pattern was just what the guidance program needed to meet the needs of a student body with many diverse needs. With this new system each of the four counselors could do what they did best and act as a team. The personal counselor also teamed up with the school nurse, the psychologist, and the social worker, all of whom met once a week with the school administrators to review students in need and pinpoint a plan for intervention. There were no weak links in this process; rather, there were many open doors that students, staff, and parents could walk through to get help. Every member of this team had a role to play and a special expertise readily available when needed.

The kind of intervention described here works best in large schools where there are large numbers of counselors available for this differentiated staffing model. Unfortunately, the vast majority of high schools still assign students to counselors by grade or alphabet, instead of by the needs of students and the skills of counselors, as this case study highlights.

However, in smaller schools where there may be only one or two counselors, the approach needs to be different. In this situation, counselors need to reach out and train teachers, students, support staff, administrators, parents, and community members as helpers. One counselor in a school cannot do it all, that is, do college-admission counseling, scheduling, testing, and career counseling. However, they can empower and train a team of helpers to work alongside them.

As I explore in "Combating Student Tobacco Addiction in Secondary Schools,"[1] why use the secondary schools as prevention centers for tobacco and other substance-abuse addictions? Because that's where the students are! Here's the story of how one school used their resources to offer much-needed intervention.

In the everyday world of secondary-school life, the addictions of students are no secret. A look at suspension records for smoking, days absent, failure lists, attendance at summer school, and retention lists will show a core of students who may be addicted to tobacco and as a result are not succeeding in school. Tobacco addiction has a huge cost for teens who regularly miss class and school to feed their addiction. Conversations with administrators, counselors, secretaries in the discipline office, teachers, hallway monitors, bus drivers, and monitors who patrol the school grounds can easily identify these addicted students.

These are the people who are in daily contact with students. They know who is at risk with tobacco and other substances. Often, they want to help the at-risk student, but they don't know how. The mission of the modern secondary school is no longer solely academic. Issues of health and welfare are upon us whether we want them or not. Schools can respond to these new needs. There are things we can do and new directions to take.

What steps can be taken to help secondary schools become centers for prevention and early intervention?

- Step 1: Reconceptualize response to addicted students. Develop a program with staff and parents to plan alternatives to present school policy. For example, addicted students will have the opportunity to enter a smoking support program instead of suspension.
- Step 2: Staffing. Identify key staff members who can develop and implement intervention efforts with addicted students.
- Step 3: Identification. Identify those students who need early intervention for tobacco addiction.
- Step 4: Create conditions for intervention. Develop trust and communication with addicted students by key school personnel.
- Step 5: Understand the problems. Involve addicted students in planning their own recovery programs. Learn from addicted students how they began smoking, what smoking does for them (i.e., relief from pressures of school), their view of themselves and their world, concerns about their health, the relationship of smoking to other substance abuse, and the role of parents and friends in this addiction. We must know how it all began before we can help.
- Step 6: Intervention. Provide the necessary education, support, counseling, and referral to help addicted students reduce or stop smoking. For example:

  - teaching specific techniques to relax without a cigarette;
  - teaching techniques to resist pressures to smoke;
  - building up confidence and competence;
  - building up general health awareness (weight, blood pressure, cholesterol);
  - developing sources of support in the school where addicted students can go on a regular basis;
  - developing easy access to additional counseling and rehab placement for other substance-abuse problems;
  - developing support networks for addicted students in the evenings and on weekends;
  - involving parents (when involvement will help the process).

How would this six-step plan actually work? What follows is a case study of the development and implementation of a five-hour-a-day smoking-reduction program at Shoreham Wading River High School on the north shore of Long Island by myself, the student-assistance counselor at the school, and school nurse Lorraine Esper. It is hoped that this case study will provide a road map for other secondary schools in their efforts to help addicted students.

THE SCHOOL

Shoreham Wading River High School has been a leader in education at the local, state, and national level for the past fifteen years. The school has pioneered educational innovations in a number of areas such as an advisory program in which teachers serve as advisors to small groups of students in house groups, community-service projects, untracked curricula, athletic programs for all students, no department chairpersons, parent conferences in which grades are reported in person by the teacher-advisor, and a marvelous special education program.

The school's athletic, library, computer and technology resource, and fine arts facilities serve as an important back-up for an innovative and creative staff. A large percentage of professional staff hold doctorate degrees. Parents are proud of the school and often cite the school district as the main reason they moved to Shoreham.

Students are proud of Shoreham Wading River High School as well. The average daily attendance for the six-hundred-plus students is over 97 percent. This is a school where the needs of the students are valued. Each student belongs to a house group made up of eight to ten other students in the same grade level. House groups meet each morning for fifteen minutes for support and information. The house group teacher also meets with his or her students in individual conferences and advises students on personal, health, and well-being issues, course selection, and college and vocational choice. The house group teacher is the center of the helping process and serves as the primary referral source to the personal counselor and source of contact for parents.

The curriculum has been developed to meet the needs of students without tracking. More than one hundred students are in special education programs, but are mainstreamed in many classes. Approximately twenty students are in an alternative program that has a strong focus on outdoor education. Computers are located in large numbers throughout the building.

A weight-training room is open each afternoon and evening for students, parents, and community members. The community library is housed adjacent to the school. Many citizens are in positive daily contact with the students, as they use both the weight room and the library. Over 80 percent of the students are involved in sports programs.

Finally, there is a great deal of support for personal development and counseling. House group teachers receive special training in the helping process. There are three guidance counselors, a student-assistance counselor, a school psychologist, and a part-time social worker. There is plenty of support available for students. While no institution is perfect, Shoreham Wading River High School is a school that really works to educate and improve the lives of its students. It is a school where innovation and new ideas can take hold.

THE PROBLEM

However, students in Shoreham, like all other communities in America, do have problems. Many parents move to attractive suburban communities expecting their children to grow up untarnished by the world and accepted by the best colleges. However, life's problems have a way of finding parent and children even in the so-called best communities. It's not the fairy tale they envisioned. In communities like Shoreham, there is tremendous pressure on students to make the "right" decisions about college selection, careers, friendships, relationships, and risky behaviors. Life is not simple for today's adolescent.

With the pressure comes a great need for relief. Students often turn to alcohol, drugs, and tobacco for this relief despite what is taught in health classes. Alcohol and tobacco are easily available, and they are cheaper than going to a movie. Students who turn to tobacco are more visible as they act out, skip class and school, and challenge the school's authority to play by the rules. Some so-called well-behaved "good kids" and athletes also turn to tobacco, alcohol, and drugs for relief but they do it quietly, below the school's radar, until their abuse gets out of hand. They may be harder to help because they hide their secret addictions.

In the search for relief, some students avoid real harm, while a few become addicted. When students become addicted, they bring their problems and habits into the schools. And when students are troubled, so are teachers, administrators, counselors, and other support staff. The schools must be prepared to deal with these troubled students.

There are three simple truths that underline the need for prevention and intervention programs in the schools:

1. Some students will become addicted to tobacco, alcohol, and drugs while in high school. Drug-free communities only exist in a fantasy world.
2. These addicted students will bring their problems into the school.
3. The school should be prepared to intervene to create conditions in which these addicted students can break their habit.

Students who were addicted to tobacco in Shoreham brought their addiction into the high school. They smoked before school and between classes in bathrooms and outside. They numbered between twenty-five and thirty-five. This small number of students represented a challenge for many groups in the school. For health teachers and proponents of wellness education, their continuing abuse of tobacco was a daily reminder of the power of addiction and the failed effort, as they perceived it, of their work. For administrators, the smokers meant a continual game of cat and mouse—finding the smokers, suspending them, and then going through the same process the next day.

These administrators also felt the heat of critics in the community who felt the school was lax in its efforts to stop "the smoking problem." For fellow students, the smokers represented a group who were consciously choosing to damage their health and shorten their lives, a group to be avoided.

THE STUDENT-ASSISTANCE COUNSELOR

Shoreham Wading River High School decided to implement a student-assistance counseling program based on the student-assistance model developed by the Hazelden Institute in Center City, Minnesota. I was selected to be the counselor. The project would be part of the guidance and counseling program. The main thrust was to assist students troubled by physical, emotional, legal, sexual, medical, family, and chemical-use problems.

During the first two years of the project, more than 150 students were seen in individual and group counseling each year. Many of the students in the smoker group were involved in counseling. I developed a close and trusting relationship with many of them. I had established myself in the school as one of the key helpers.

When school opened in September, the principal asked me to come up with a new approach to help students who were addicted to tobacco. It was agreed that suspensions were not solving anything. I suggested asking the school nurse to meet with me and some members of the smoking group to plan together a program that would help students to reduce or stop smoking. I felt the nurse would be a critical part of the project. Her office was adjacent to mine, and many of the smokers sought her out for advice and counseling. They trusted and respected her.

We decided we would informally invite each of the smokers in the school to a get-together with doughnuts and soda where we would ask them to help plan a program that would assist any student interested in cutting back or stopping smoking.

We were not targeting specific individuals. Participation would be voluntary, with a built-in incentive of released time from some classes. The smoking group would be the leaders in the project. This was their area of expertise. When we approached the students, they were thrilled at the idea of being involved , even asking if they could invite friends. For many of these students, this was the first time in their school career they had been asked to take a leadership role. By the time of our first planning meeting, thirty students had volunteered to help plan a smoking-reduction project.

INVOLVING ADDICTED STUDENTS

We held three planning meetings with the smoking group "consultants." Prior to the planning, we met with staff members and asked for their feedback. Released time was provided for the students, and funds were made available for coffee, doughnuts, soda, and lollipops to suck on to reduce the ever-present urge to smoke. To our surprise, the lollipops were a big hit. As the sessions began, we were overwhelmed by the students' willingness to talk about their smoking and addiction. Many reported it was the first time they had the opportunity to talk about their concerns with smoking. Their comments provided the basis for building our project.

Here is what we learned about the tobacco addiction of these students.

- Most had started smoking in middle school in grades 6 and 7.
- They did not perform well in school. Many had repeated a grade or attended summer school.
- They did not feel they were part of the school, and felt isolated from other students who were into sports and health.
- They looked to each other for support and socialization.
- They shared a negative view of their future. They had little hope of getting to college or getting a good job.
- They were concerned about their general health. Many felt they were not in good physical shape (overweight, high blood pressure, coughing). They felt they would not live a long life.
- They reported addictions to other substances, such as alcohol.
- Many reported that they wanted to cut back or stop smoking, but had failed each time they tried. They felt great pressure from other group members to keep smoking.
- They enjoyed the game of trying to hide and outwit school administrators. The game made school more fun for them.

PLANNING THE INTERVENTION PROGRAM

At the third planning meeting, we asked the group what they thought would help addicted students to cut back or stop smoking. Here's what they said:

- Focus on helping students get through the school day without smoking or cutting back so they don't get suspended.
- Have ongoing groups, similar to the planning meetings, where students could talk about their addictions and learn new ways to relax. The groups should be no larger than ten students.
- Have a place, like the nurse's office, where they could leave their cigarettes in the morning so they wouldn't be tempted. Have lollipops available.

The nurse suggested that we call the project the Five Hour a Day Project, because our primary focus was on helping students get through the school day without smoking. Our target area was from 8 a.m. to 1 p.m. Twenty-seven of the thirty students volunteered to participate. They divided themselves into three smaller groups. The plan was for each group to meet with us once a week for six weeks.

Each student would be asked to keep a daily record of how many cigarettes they were smoking and the times and places they smoked. What was their pattern? What stresses triggered their need to smoke? This material would be shared at the weekly sessions. They were also asked to sign a contract to which they made a commitment to try to cut back or stop smoking and to complete the program.

Each of the six sessions would have a major theme. These were:

- Who's in charge of your smoking? This session would focus on how we consciously arrive at the decision to smoke, how we can reevaluate this decision, and some next steps that can help us to cut back or stop. Homework would be to make a verbal commitment to another group member to try not to smoke during school hours.
- Self-image: This session would focus on how smoking has become a major part of our self-image. Why do we need tobacco? What does it do for us? How does tobacco harm us? What kind of self-image do we want? Homework would be to observe how we view ourselves as students, sons or daughters, friends, and community members.
- Stress factors and trigger mechanisms: This session would focus on those things that trigger the desire to smoke and the exploration of alternative reactions. Homework would be to try out new behaviors.
- The power of addiction: This session would focus on the power of the tobacco and other addictions and how we begin to break long-formed habits. The emphasis here is small gains with much praise. Homework would be to observe how changing habits is a slow process with many failures. Homework would focus on alternative ways we can reward and support ourselves.

- Rewarding ourselves in other ways: This session would focus on what we want out of life: our dreams, hopes, what has meaning and importance for us, and how we've become disappointed in ourselves and used substances to hide the pain and failure. Homework would focus on alternative ways we can reward, support, and like/love ourselves.
- What have we learned? This session would review the data. Have we been able to reduce our smoking or cut back? Have we had fewer suspensions? Have we learned what stresses trigger our smoking? Have we learned alternatives that we can use when stress strikes? Have we learned about our self-image and how we can improve and feel better about ourselves? Have we learned that changing an addiction is a slow process, filled with many failures? Have we learned where the sources of support are in school and in the community? Have we learned where the danger areas are for us as we begin to recover from tobacco addiction?

HOW THE PROGRAM WORKED

- All twenty-seven of the volunteer group members attended each session and completed the program.
- Of the twenty-seven participants, five stopped smoking, seventeen cut back, and five made no change.
- Daily attendance increased for the students in the group.
- Only two students were given detention for smoking during the program.
- Two students went into rehab for alcohol abuse as a direct result of participation in the project.
- Students in the group became involved in more ongoing personal counseling with the student-assistance counselor.
- Students became more conscious of their health and worked with the school nurse in areas related to weight, sexuality, and nutrition.
- Students developed a booklet of hints to use in stopping smoking. This booklet included the following suggestions:

  - Leave cigarettes where you can't easily get them; pick them up at the end of the day.
  - Bring only two cigarettes to school and make a promise not to borrow from others.
  - Do not go to places where you can smoke. Instead, go to the health office, the library, or to a friend who will encourage you not to smoke.
  - When under stress, take a deep breath and visualize a peaceful scene like a sunset.
  - If you have a free period, go for a walk without a cigarette.

- Keep putting off that cigarette, one hour at a time, until it becomes easier to go a longer time.
- Find ways to occupy your mind and hands. Read, meditate, suck on a lollipop, even do homework. Keep busy.
- Tell your friends that your goal is to cut back or stop, not to get detention, and not to get suspended. Make a commitment.

- Because of the success of the five-hour project, the student-assistance counselor started a forty-eight-hour group to help students get through the weekends without drinking alcohol, smoking, and abusing other drugs. Some of the participants in the five-hour project served as leaders for this group.
- Students in the group became involved with parents in helping organize TALK (talking to your child in a loving way), forums that helped educate parents about real issues in adolescent life.
- Students in the group put on a play for elementary/middle school students and parent/community groups on how to create a smoke-free world.
- Students in the group presented a workshop on the five-hour project for Suffolk County guidance counselors.
- Students in the group presented a workshop on the project at the annual high school staff awareness day.
- A local paper reported on the project. A little fame came their way. They were no longer just "dirt bags" and "smokers." Their parents read something positive about their children for a change.
- At the end of the project, the district sponsored a dinner for the participants at a local restaurant to reward the group for their pioneering work. Each student received a certificate indicating successful completion of the program.

The five-hour project was offered again the spring and fall of 1991, and the spring of 1992. Many of the core group remained as leader-participants and recruited new students. Approximately fifty students participated over the two-year period. I left the school in June 1992.

CONCLUSION

This was a successful project. It was developed by students and staff members working together. It helped students reduce or stop smoking. It helped raise self-esteem and increase overall health awareness. More students became involved in personal counseling and rehab, and became leaders in forums for their peers, parents, and educators. The school was willing to take a new approach to tobacco addiction, and it worked, far beyond the original vision.

There are two major lessons here: First, schools can intervene to help addicted students by utilizing existing personnel and resources in different ways. In the five-hour-a-day project, the school nurse became a group leader and teacher as well as a nurse. She was able to utilize the full range of her professional skills. In the process, everyone benefited. Second, helping oneself and helping others is a powerful part of the recovery process. Many addicted students are looking for a way out of their addiction. Programs that are built with a keen awareness of the students' own needs and concerns can work. Things can change.

The final chapter will outline a differentiated staffing model that enables personal counselors to find a way to provide the entire school community with intervention when they fall on troubled times. This model is based on the notion that every member of the school community, not just the students at the margins of school life, can be at risk and need supportive intervention. Personal counselors cannot perform these needed interventions alone. There are too many problems to be solved in our large high schools.

Therefore, this staffing model involves bringing staff, students, parents, administrators, and community resources on board as helpers, thereby establishing a helping community in which each member has a helping role to fulfill when they observe a member heading for trouble.

In the real school world, this communitywide intervention process may not be perfect and the reality is not every member will be onboard with the helping role. However, it is a role in which the personal counselor trains and calls on each member to be aware that they indeed have helping skills that are welcomed and needed. They no longer have to look the other way in silence when they observe a troubled member.

Their role is to act; intervene; seek the help and advice of the personal counselor, school nurse, social worker, school psychologist, or principal; and serve in a supportive role until help is on the way and secured. In this process, the school community is creating a "circle of wellness" that reduces anonymity and asks each member to take notice and act when trouble strikes.

In the real world some schools will not have a personal counselor, school social worker, or school psychologist, but many have a "go to" person who can enlist the helping skills of staff, students, parents, administrators, and community resources. One caring, skilled staff member can empower an entire school community.

The personal counselor and "go to" staff member are at the center of this circle of the wellness intervention process. By reaching out and training every member of the school community as helpers, they create a culture that is ready and set to offer intervention. In doing so, they help develop trust, respect, and quality communication with every group in the school, thereby reducing barriers, isolation, and anonymity and establishing a "we are all in this together" culture.

Mutual respect, trust, and quality communication don't happen overnight or without many examples of skillful interventions when and where they are needed. Reports don't make it happen, only real stories/proof do, so that all members of the community can "see," understand, and come to believe that when they are troubled, their school counselor, teachers, peers, support staff, and administrator will deliver help and support them. As in family life, trust and respect must be earned by participating in good deeds that are observed and internalized by every member of family, not just words muttered at PTA workshops, church sermons, or in a book of ten steps to a wholesome family life.

NOTE

1. William L. Fibkins, "Combating Student Tobacco Addiction in Secondary Schools," *NASSP Bulletin* 177, no. 557 (December 1993): 51–59.

Chapter Eight

Personal Counselors Cannot Solve All the Problems of Troubled Students

They Need Skilled Allies to Join Their Effort

New York Times reporter Kirsten Hohenadel's piece[1] about Fred Rogers of the PBS show "Mr. Rogers Neighborhood" points out that in his measured cadence of his familiar voice, he spread the unconditional love. "You've made this day a special day, just by being you. There is no person in the whole world like you, and I like you, just the way you are."

Counselors need a lot of Mr. Rogers's unconditional love even though, being human, it doesn't always come easy. It's easy to care and help students with whom we are safe, comfortable, and connected. The hard work comes with caring and loving students who resist our help, who threaten us, and whose backgrounds, culture, and behaviors are very different from our own. We need to be our own counselor and accept our feelings and, more importantly, make sure we create a helping system that is absent of places we can hide and avoid our mandate to help each student and "like them just the way they are."

Hohenadel describes Rogers as feeling both vulnerable and safe at the same time in trying to connect with young people, feelings that best describe the way counselors "should" feel as they approach students in need. Successful counselors have a little of Rogers in them. Rogers's philosophy of the best way to relate to young people is simple and clear: "Deep and simple is far more essential than shallow and complex."

Good advice to model as an effective school counseling delivery system whose goal, like Rogers's, is to guide the school community through the ups and downs of childhood and who creates a theme, like Rogers's signature song, "Won't You Be in My Neighborhood?," which provides a hearty welcoming for every student. Like Rogers's use of TV, we need to use the schools in the most thoughtful and measured way to be helpful to children and their families, never to exploit them. Like many teachers and counselors, Rogers came to his mission of caring so much about the well-being of children after being bullied as a shy, overweight boy.

As he describes in his book, *Life's Journeys According to Mister Rogers*[2]:

> When I was a kid, I was shy and overweight. I was a perfect target for ridicule. One day (how well I remember that day, and it's more than sixty years ago!) we got out of school early, and I started to walk home by myself. It wasn't long before I sensed I was being followed by a whole group of boys.

> As I walked faster, I looked around, and they started to call my name and came close and closer and got louder and louder," Freddy, hey, fat Freddy. We are going to get you, fat Freddy." I resented those kids for not seeing beyond my fatness or my shyness. And I didn't know that it was all right to resent it, to feel bad about it, even to feel very sad. I didn't know it was all right to feel any of those things, because the advice I got from grown-ups was, 'Just let on you don't care, then nobody will bother you.'

> What I actually did was mourn. I cried to myself whenever I was alone. I cried through my fingers as I made up songs on the piano. I sought out stories of other people who were poor in spirit, and I felt for them. I started to look behind the things that people did and said and little by little concluded that Saint-Exupery was absolutely right when he wrote in The Little Prince, "What is essential is invisible to the eye."

> So after a lot of sadness, I began a lifelong search for what is essential. I don't know how this came to me, maybe through one of my teachers or from my grandfather, who used to say to me after we had a visit together, "Freddy, you made this day a special day for me." My hunch is all those extraordinary, ordinary people who believed that I was more than I thought I was, all those saints who helped a fat, shy kid to see more clearly what was really essential.

Rogers was lucky. Lucky in the sense that he found his niche with his teachers and his grandfather, who told him, "I'm proud of you. I'm proud of you. I hope that you're as proud as I am, that you're learning how important you are. Learning how important each person you see can be. Discovering each one's specialty is the most important learning. I'm proud of you. I'm proud of you. I hope that you are proud of you too."

Rogers says he was helped to find his faith by "all those extraordinary and ordinary people who believed that I was more than I thought I was, all those saints who helped a fat, shy, kid to see more clearly what was really essential."

That many "extraordinary and ordinary people" helped Rogers to find "his" path and search for what was essential to him in life has valuable lessons for the personal counselor if he is to be successful in reaching out to all those students who have lead a difficult life like Rogers. That message is that making a major impact on helping the large number of students in our large high schools will require the help and skills of many "extraordinary and ordinary" people who can help them believe that they are more than they thought.

That means enlisting skilled teachers, students, administrators, support staff, parents, and community helping resources as allies and partners in a schoolwide helping process. As Rogers suggests, "There's a part of all of us that longs to know that even what's weakest about us is still redeemable and can ultimately count for something good, every human being has value. This is the basis of all healthy relationships. Through living each day as it is given to me, I've learned that it cannot be 'taught,' but it can be 'caught' from those who live their lives right alongside of us. What a privilege to be able to look for the good in our neighbors."

And our neighbors in the schools are the students, staff, administrators, and parents. The goal of a caring school is for us all to become neighbors who watch out and care for each other. But as Rogers suggests, that's something that cannot be "taught"; it has to be "caught" from those who live their lives right alongside caring students, teachers, support staff, administrators, and parents who don't look the other way when they observe a member of "their" school community heading toward the margins of school life.

Rather, they act because they feel their helping role is essential to the overall well-being of its members. In this helping role they are finding what is "essential" in their lives and that is "catching" a troubled person before it's too late. In this helping process, counselors need to invite in and sell other members of the school community on the need to help them open up a new path for students, of being their brothers' and sisters' keepers, so students aren't left, as Rogers was early on, to "cry to myself whenever I was alone."

Many troubled students like Fred Rogers arrive at their schools each morning in search of a caring adult and peers to tell them they have value and count for something, adults and peers who can help them believe that they are worth more than their own low self-perception. They need to be "caught" early on before their troubles succeed in ruining their lives. In order to succeed, we need an intervention system that is ready and set to intervene and calls on the helping roles of counselors, students, teachers, administrators, support staff, and parents.

Here are some examples of what each group in their school can contribute to an intervention system with many open doors for help.

COUNSELORS

Counselors can redesign their intervention systems and make personal counseling a top priority. The world has changed and new systems are needed. Counselors now need to forge a new role that enables them to be in the forefront in efforts to train staff, students, and parents to be effective helpers and serve as crisis counselors—the people students and parents turn to in crisis when serious situations like suicide emerge. They need to make personal counseling easily available, attractive, and safe.

An intervention process that teens in trouble want to be involved in, a chosen destination. This new role requires enlisting and training teachers, students, support staff, administrators, and parents as natural allies and training them to acquire simple helping skills that they can use in helping students on the front lines and to make good referrals in times of crises. An effective counseling program to meet the needs of today's students then should include the following services.

The counseling program should offer individual and group counseling; awareness groups on health, personal, and safety issues such as tobacco cessation and alcohol, drug, and obesity issues; peer-counseling training for students and parents to provide them with skills to help, accept, and understand their troubled peers; and leadership training for students in order to help them create a caring environment in the school that fosters a commitment to being our brothers' keeper.

The program should establish clear pathways for students who need referral, rehab and hospitalization, and a smooth/caring reentry to school; summer camps for at-risk students on building self-esteem, health promotion, and physical activity; weekend support groups for students and parents who may be at risk; and ongoing training for teachers, students, support staff, administrators, and parents to be effective helpers.

Will some counselors resist this holistic counseling approach? Of course, resistance to change runs deep. Some counselors will resist giving up their helping turf. Some staff members will resist taking on a helping role, saying "it's not my job"; some parents and students will resist staff members acting as "counselors" and some administrators will resist this new helping role for staff, suggesting that it's too "risky." Strong and persuasive leadership and an ongoing sales job will be required in order for staff, administrators, parents, students, and community members to decide to play a proactive role in helping troubled teens.

The program should include a sales campaign that helps convince counselors and administrators to give up on the obsolete practice of assigning counselors by grade or alphabet and develop a new organization that assigns counselors by skills and need, specific assignments for personal counseling, college selection, class placement, etc. It will not be an easy road.

As identified in chapter 3, counselors who are safe and comfortable with a quasi-administrator role will resist, calling a new configuration of counselor roles names like "ludicrous," "bizarre," and "emotionally saturated for personal counselors." And that's tame stuff. When people are asked to change, things can get very rough and those leading a change effort had better be prepared to have their professional and personal lives vilified.

The basic question for counselors is not when but how to respond to the needs of troubled teens. This book proposes such a model, embodied in the personal counselor's role. The voices of counselor leaders at the local, state, and national level who are proponents of the ASCA national model's "responsive services," which address student's direct, immediate concerns and include counseling, consultation, referral, and systems support, need to be heard loud and clear and they need to be prepared to guide the now-necessary changes to implementation.

Failure to respond will result in maintaining a failed counseling system for both counselors and students. In the end this kind of necessary change is highly political. It requires well-informed and courageous counselor and administrative leaders to single out the most resisting and vocal counselors, teachers, parents, and community members and win them over.

They should be won over with a face-to-face sales campaign focused on *why* change is now needed, *why* their positive participation is required, and *why* a new counselor organization will make for an improved intervention system that is responsive to the concerns of students, parents, and staff members—a system in every member of the school community that is prepared to act so no members fall between the cracks.

Meeting critics face to face in conversation, even confrontation, is after all a political process in which resisters can be challenged, not allowed to escape responsibility for their position or seek cover, and gently, sometimes aggressively, persuaded to get on board. Most change projects fail because charges by resisters go unanswered and allowed to dominate the change landscape. Meeting resisters head on, face to face, in dialogue allows an opportunity to meet common ground. Avoiding a personal/professional dialogue is a sure way to bring about failure.

STUDENTS

Students who are troubled or headed for trouble are known to other students. Yet the culture of our schools often stresses that troubled teens should only be helped by trained counselors. However, this process robs caring teens of the many opportunities they have to help and direct troubled peers to sources of help where they can begin to rebuild their lives. It leaves them as onlookers, passive observers, not responsible for peers who are making cries for help.

This is not saying teens should be counselors for their peers. But they can learn through peer counseling specific helping and referring skills that allow them to intervene and be useful. We need to remember that helping another person can be a very simple and rewarding event. Simple overtures can serve as a lifesaver to troubled teens. For example, "How are things going? Have you thought about getting help? Let's go down and make an appointment with Dr. Jones. He is a good helper," works best.

No, not every overture goes smoothly but it can open a door for self-awareness. These overtures and invitations to help are doable by every student in a helping school community. And we need to remember that not all at-risk and troubled teens are school failures, hostile and acting out. We need to be cognizant that the best and the brightest athletes, actors, musicians, etc., have unique pressures.

Ironically, because they are the so-called best and brightest, going to Harvard, etc., they are not supposed to have problems. But they, as we all do, have problems and often keep them hidden. Students with a 4.0 GPA as a rule don't show cracks until it's too late. A caring and skilled peer can encourage them to get help. Getting help is okay and acceptable for all!

No, not every student will embrace a helping role at first. It's new territory for them to be seen as a vital cog in the school's intervention system. Many students in our schools, like our communities, are separated along racial, economic, and cultural lines. Cliques abound. Administrators, counselors, teachers, parents, and student leaders will have to sell students on the notion that it is important in a caring school community that they try to help and be of use to peers at risk.

When they ask, "What's in it for me?," they can be told they will feel more useful, responsible, involved, and learn how to accept and understand peers who may be different and troubled. Training students to be helpers is an important role for the personal counselor.

TEACHERS

Teachers are on the front lines. They are often the first adults to observe a student headed for trouble. The symptoms of a troubled life are easily and painfully observed: a bruised face, lateness, absenteeism, poor attention, little self-care, no parent support, hangovers after the weekend, and dramatic change in behavior such as being a 4.0 student then suddenly becoming depressed and withdrawn.

But teachers can't help and be expected to help if they are untrained. And they can't be expected to help and be a front-line resource just by saying "you should help these troubled kids." Words are cheap. Training requires resources. The age-old saying, "I'm just a teacher. . . . I'm not trained to help kids," has some wisdom in it. Encouraging teachers to help but offering them little or no training can only lead to mischief and failure.

What we need to be about is viewing teachers as a primary resource in our battle to help teens and give them the training and skills to get the job done—that is, to be well prepared, ready and set, confident they can help, and when necessary refer, when they see one of their students in need.

No, not every teacher will welcome this new helping role. Many will say they are academic teachers and not hired to be advisors or quasi-counselors. This response might have been acceptable in the 1950s but times have changed and well-trained teachers are needed to help the growing number of troubled teens. Times changed and roles need to change. Isn't it better to train teachers and prepare them to help than to leave them on their own, untrained? We don't send soldiers off to war without extensive basic training.

Clearly encouraging teachers to use their natural helping skills and acquire new, simple, helping skills is doable in every school. They can be taught how to intervene and offer help, make good referrals to reputable sources of help in the school and community, and to share their concerns about students with colleagues and administrators so they have support. This is not to say that teachers should play a messiah role. But they can serve as an ongoing source of help for students who appear out of sync, not well, confused, and looking for a helping hand. Helping is not rocket science.

Every teacher can acquire simple helping skills that make intervention more comfortable for them and enhance their teaching role. For example, teachers who acquire effective helping skills become more effective teachers because they no longer avoid those troubled students who appear hostile and disinterested in their classes. As learners, teachers will maximize their impact by learning how to avoid turning their back on troubled teens, looking the other way, and begin interacting with them in new ways that get them on board as healthy and committed students. Training and supporting teachers to be helpers is an important role for personal counselors.

ADMINISTRATORS

Administrators need to be known as the chief helpers in their schools—a new and, for some, strange role. Some will ask, "Aren't administrators supposed to put forth a tough and forceful role model?" Surely administrators need to be tough and forceful but today's schools call for leaders who are committed to developing a schoolwide intervention system in which no student will fall through the cracks. No easy task. But creating conditions in which counselors, teachers, support staff, and parents work as natural allies to help students goes a long way. An intervention process in which everyone in the school community is asked to be accountable and responsible for each other's well-being raises expectations.

As such, the school administrator first needs to see himself as a positive role model for the helping process. As the school's lead teacher, he needs to model how to intervene and help troubled teens. He needs to use the whole playing field to communicate his expectations that every member of the school community is expected to help students with their personal and non-academic problems. His presence, behaviors, and actions model his new role: for example, leadership at faculty meetings, supervision sessions, team meetings, assemblies, extracurricular events, and parent and community meetings. He rewards students, teachers, staff members, and parents whom he observes in successful helping roles. He gives needed attention to the value of a schoolwide helping culture in a healthy school climate.

No, not every administrator will embrace this role. Administrators have a lot on their plate. Some will say, "Now they want me to model effective helping skills. What's next?" But like it or not, helping troubled teens has become a top priority and the school administrator's task is to get the job done. It behooves him to begin to learn effective helping skills and set expectations for staff so that they, too, will be held accountable for personal interventions.

Besides, who's better at taking the lead in an intervention system to show teachers how to reach teens headed for failure and trouble? People listen, learn, and act when the boss gets personally involved.

SUPPORT STAFF

Support staff, such as secretaries, monitors, and custodians, are ideally positioned to help troubled teens. They, like teachers and students, are on the front lines and can easily observe a teen at risk. They often hold a position of great trust by teens who view them as allies, not professionals. Teens can share their story while hanging out in the lunch room or the back of the school. Sensitive and well-trained support staff can pick up the clues of a troubled life and quickly direct a student to a reputable source of help.

As with teacher and student helpers, simple words work best. "How are things? Did you know Dr. Jones is starting a helping group at 2:30 on Tuesday? I'll walk you there if you are afraid. I read in the paper your Mom got arrested for DWI. What's happening at home? Must be hard on you knowing the news is all over the school." To their advantage, support staff don't have professional degrees. But they are often people who care about students and have a natural intimate relationship that can open doors for help.

Sometimes being a nonprofessional has advantages for the troubled teens. Support staff members are often jargon free, street-smart, and are from the local neighborhoods. They know and understand teens and families on an intimate basis and are free of the burden of too much schooling and training. They are simply caring people just trying to help. However, they are often left out of the intervention process, although in the everyday life of students they play a huge role. They need to be included as allies and provided with the necessary training and support needed to make them "legitimate" helpers in the eyes of staff members, students, and parents.

PARENTS

Parents can be a significant source of help for troubled teens. With limited training that focuses on adolescent development and how to help a teen headed for trouble, many parents can easily become credible sources of help and referral. I am not talking specifically about parents helping their own child, but, rather, I am stressing that parents in neighborhoods observe troubled teens every day. In fact, every neighborhood, regardless of economics, class, and culture, has kids in need.

Effective training can help parents not scorn or be fearful of these teens and their parents. Rather, training will help them reach out to these teens and parents and be ready and set to offer support and sources of referral. They will learn not to look the other way and understand that the teens and parents in trouble could easily be them at some other time in their lives. After all, we are all at risk at some point and need support and guidance to make a successful transition. We are more alike than different. Parents have also been left out of the helping process, although they often play huge roles in helping troubled teens.

The time has come to create new pathways and open up new doors to help troubled teens and their parents. We need to see everyone in the school community as a potential helper and source of referral. Much of this effort needs to focus on administrators, counselors, teachers, students, support staff, and parent leaders who understand, without blame and acrimony, that the current intervention system doesn't work and needs reengineering.

Counselors, if they are to maintain a leadership and proactive role in the schools, need to begin to offer a variety of new training and counseling services that can ready students, teachers, support staff, administrators, and parents to be effective helpers. Administrators need to provide the role model, resources, and support for this new training and the personal counseling role to emerge as a critical and needed service. Our times require that expectations be raised to meet the rising tide of personal problems our teens are bringing into the schools.

Without these necessary changes, our secondary schools will limp along accepting a flawed intervention system and failure as a normal part of school life—going through the motions of help yet knowing it doesn't really work for kids, educators, and parents, a little like a husband and wife in a marriage that doesn't work staying together, somehow hoping things will change, get better. But they never do.

The bottom line is accepting the reality that teens' problems are increasing and the one doable solution is to demystify and share the helping process so teachers, students, support staff, administrators, and parents can serve as well-trained backups for the personal counselors whose new role will be that of trainer and counselor for the most in-need students. It's called maximizing our resources.

This schoolwide helping model with many open doors for help is very much like "Mr. Rogers' Neighborhood," in which children and adults are well known, connected, valued, cared for, and encouraged to have dreams, aspirations, and hope. Unfortunately many of our high school students come from families that are not connected to their neighbors and community. In a sense, many lack a helping community they can turn to when trouble strikes.

There is often no one to call, tell your story to, or get support when the bottom falls out of your life. As Dr. Seuss says, "You'll come to a place where the streets are not marked. Some windows are lighted. But mostly they are dark. Do you dare to stay out? Do you dare go in? You can get so confused."

As Robert Putnam[3] suggests, there has been an erosion of America's social connectedness and community involvement over the last several decades. First, the American family structure has changed in several important and relevant ways. The downturn in civic engagement coincided with the breakdown of the traditional family unit: Mom, Dad, and the kids; the family itself is, by some accounts, a key form of social capital, and perhaps its eclipse is part of the explanation for the reduction of joining and trusting the wider community.

Putnam suggests that the evidence of a loosening of family bonds is unequivocal. The century-long increase in divorce rates and the more-recent increases in one-parent families have resulted in the doubling of one-parent households since 1950. Putnam says that the fraction of adults who are married and have students at home, the archetypal Ozzie and Harriet, was sliced by more than one-third, from 40 percent in 1970 to 26 percent in 1997. The traditional family unit is down a lot.

Putnam suggests that there are other factors also that have contributed to the decline in civic engagement and social capital. Here are some of those factors.

1. There has been an erosion of social capital over the last several decades. That is a decline in the norms and networks of norms and reciprocity that foster collective action. It's the friendship, professional circles, clubs, neighborhoods, churches, and alumni organizations where you help the group or fellow members because you care about and trust the group and know your actions will ultimately benefit all.
2. Pressure of time and money, including the special pressures on two-career families, contributed measurably to the diminution of our social and community involvement. The fraction of married Americans who definitely say, "Our whole family usually eats together," has declined a third from about 50 percent to 34 percent in just the last two decades.
3. The increase in movement to the suburbs and creation of unattractive sprawling landscapes also played a supporting role in this process.
4. The effect of electronic entertainment, almost all television, on our leisure time has been substantial. Students are part of the TV generation.
5. Decline in PTA membership over the past several decades reflects many parents' disengagement from their children's schooling. PTAs nationwide plummeted from a membership high in the early 1960s of almost fifty members per one hundred families with school-age children to less than twenty members per one hundred in 1997.
6. Generalized trust also has evaporated. While 55 percent of American adults in 1960 believed others could be trusted most or all of the time, only 30 percent did in 1998, and the future looks bleaker because the decline was the sharpest among our nation's youth.

Putnam's research doesn't offer a pretty or hopeful picture of the barriers facing the healthy development of today's youth. He observes that a considerable amount of research dating back at least fifty years has demonstrated that trust, networking, and norms of reciprocity within a child's family, school, peer groups, and larger community have wide-ranging effects on the child's opportunities and choices, and hence, on his behavior and development.

As seen above, the emergence of two-career and one-parent families, pressures on time and money, longer commutes to work, and the increase in passive TV watching have led to a decline in parental involvement with children's school and an increase in the amount of time children are on their own and vulnerable to others' behaviors. As Putnam suggests, when parents are involved in their children's education, children do better in school and the schools themselves are better. But when parents are absent, who is to fill in?

The result, as Thomas H. Sanders and Robert D. Putnam suggest[4] is accounting isolation. We are bowling alone. Sanders and Putnam observe that while a record number of Americans bowl today, bowling in organized leagues has plunged 40 percent from 1980 to 1993. They point out that the civic watering holes, such as bowling leagues, fraternal organizations, choral societies, and thousands of other places where Americans regularly met fellow citizens, talked periodically about issues of civic importance, and learned to trust others and work together are drying up.

They say much of the decline in civic connectedness is generational. Today's children (and their parents) are much less engaged in community life than their grandparents' cohort. Sanders and Putnam suggest that establishing mentoring programs is one way to close this decline.

What are the implications for teachers? As Sanders and Putnam suggest, every child needs an adult to play Batman to his or her Robin, someone who can coach, provide a "toolbox," and ultimately protect. They need adults who can share their passions with kids. In a world where students are increasingly feeling the pressures and risks that come with the lack of connections to community and family, teachers represent the one constant adult presence they have access to in schools every day.

In a sense, this situation provides teachers with an unprecedented opportunity to coach, provide a "toolbox," and protect, to become a beacon and port in the storm as other family and community sources of support are disappearing. The trick is in helping teachers become aware of the powerful role and the gifts they can offer their students in their disconnected world. This is a role of honor that can help establish teachers as leaders in our changing communities who know how to be present in the world in which students live, fulfilling the role of being the right person at the right time when trouble visits their lives.

When many students arrive at the schoolhouse door, they are in search of finding a caring community in which they can be welcomed, known well, and have caring peers and adult role models they can count on to be in their corner. Fred Rogers describes some of the elements of such a caring community this way:

> Where would any of us be without teachers—without people who have passion for their art or science or their craft and love it right in front of us? What would any of us do without teachers passing on to us what they know is essential about life?

> Transitions are almost always signs of growth, but they can bring feelings of loss. To get somewhere new, we have to leave somewhere else behind.

> We'd all like to feel self-reliant and capable of coping with whatever adversity comes our way, but that's not how most human beings are made. It's my belief that the capacity to accept help is inseparable from the capacity to give help when our turn comes to be strong. It can sometimes be difficult to ask for

support when we need it, but having someone we can count on to stick with us through the tough times can make those times much more bearable.

We can't be expected to leave the unhappy and angry parts of ourselves at the door before coming in. We all need to feel that we can bring the whole of ourselves to the people who care about us.

As a relationship matures, you start to see that just being there for each other is the most important thing you can do, just being there to listen and be sorry for them, to be happy for them, to share all that there is to share.

All we're ever asked to do in this life is to treat our neighbor—especially our neighbor who is in need—exactly as we would hope to be treated ourselves. That's our ultimate responsibility.

Personal counselors who have established a wide web of allies as helpers are prepared to act when they see a community member in trouble and resist the urge to look the other way or mutter to themselves, "Not my job or my responsibility." The personal counselor and his allies can provide a sense of community, a caring neighborhood, for students and every member of the school community.

Helping others is a habit that can be learned. People who make a conscious decision to help those in trouble, who "catch" them before their problems worsen, are not ordered to do so; rather, they are doing it for personal reasons to help someone else.

They are part of a recognized team, an important link, as neighborhood-watch volunteers in their school neighborhood—the eyes and ears on the frontlines ready and set when troubled students appear. This helping process then can give birth to a schoolwide effort that asks members of the school community to treat, as Rogers says, our neighbors, especially our neighbor who is in need, exactly as we would hope to be treated ourselves when our turn comes.

This is an effort to remind members of the school community that we are all in this together—yes different, but equal. The major task of the personal counselor is to change the habits of members of the school community so they embrace the helper's role and don't look the other way when they observe a member heading toward the margins of school and community life. As Rogers says, "We can't really understand a person unless we have the chance of knowing who that person has been, and what that person has done, and liked and suffered and believed."

NOTES

1. Kristen Hohenadel, "Please Won't You Be My Inspiration," *New York Times*, March 18, 2012, p. 12AR.

2. Fred Rogers, *Life's Journeys According to Mister Rogers* (New York: Hyperion, 2005), 18–22, 68, 76, 91, 94 108, 109.

3. Robert D. Putnam, *Bowling Alone* (New York: Simon & Schuster, 2000), 277, 283–84, 298, 302.

4. Thomas H. Sander and Robert D. Putnam, "Rebuilding the Stock of Social Capital," *The School Administrator* 8, vol. 56 (September 1999), available online at www.aasa.org/SchoolAdministratorArticle.aspx?id=14624 (accessed March 21, 2013).

References

Anderson, Jenny. "Widespread Sexual Harassment in Grades 7 to 12." *New York Times*, November 7, 2011. Available online at www.nytimes.com/2011/11/07/education/widespread-sexual-harassment-in-grades-7-to-12-found-in-study.html?_r=0. Accessed March 21, 2013.

Associated Press. "Iowa Paper Devotes Front Page to Fighting Bullying." *Associated Press*, April 22, 2012. www.foxnews.com/us/2012/04/22/iowa-paper-devotes-front-page-to-fighting-bullying-596408376. Accessed March 21, 2013.

Associated Press. "Mother of Gay Iowa Teen Blames Suicide on School, Online Bullying: Authorities Investigating." www.foxnews.com/us/2012/04/18/iowa-mom-blames-gay-teen-son-suicide-on-school. Accessed April 23, 2012.

Bardwell, Robert. "A Plea for More Counselors." *New York Times*, October 25, 2010. Available online at http://thechoice.blogs.nytimes.com/2010/10/25/counselor-2/. Accessed March 21, 2013.

Beale, Andrew V. "Questioning Whether You Have a Contemporary School Counseling Program." *Clearing House* 78, no. 2 (2004): 73–77.

Beesley, Denise. "Teachers' Perceptions of School Counselor Effectiveness: Collaborating for Student Success." *Education* 125, no. 2 (winter 2005): 259.

Bowers, Judy, Trish Hatch, and American School Counselor Association. *The ASCA National Model: A Framework for School Counseling Programs*. Alexandria, VA: American School Counselor Association, 2005.

Brooks, David. "The Machiavellian Temptation." *New York Times*, March 2, 2012.

The College Board. "Counseling at the Crossroads." National Office of School Counseling Advocacy, 2011.

Conant, James B. *The American High School Today: A First Report to Interested Citizens*. New York: McGraw-Hill, 1959

———. *The Comprehensive High School: A Second Report to Interested Citizens*. New York: McGraw-Hill, 1967.

Dahir, Carol, and Carolyn B. Stone. "MEASURE-ing Student Success: School Counselor Accountability." *Vistas*, article 57. Available online at http://counseling.org/resources/library/vistas/vistas05/vistas05.art57.pdf. Accessed March 21, 2013.

———. "School Counselor Accountability: The Path to Social Justice and Systemic Change." *Journal of Counseling and Development* 87 (winter 2009): 12–20.

Dr. Seuss. *Oh, The Places You'll Go*. New York: Random House, 1999.

Duhigg, Charles. *The Power of Habit: Why We Do What We Do in Life and Business*. New York: Random House, 2012.

The Education Trust. "Poised to Lead: How School Counselors Can Drive College and Career Readiness." The Education Trust, December 2011. Available online at www.cadfacte.net/

poised-to-lead-how-school-counselors-can-drive-college-and-career-readiness.   Accessed March 21, 2013.

Fibkins, William L. *Angel Teachers: Educators Who Care about Troubled Teens.* Lanham, MD: Rowman & Littlefield, 2012.

———. "Combating Student Tobacco Addiction in Secondary Schools." *NASSP Bulletin* 177, no. 557 (December 1993): 51–59.

———. *An Educator's Guide to Understanding the Personal Side of Students' Lives.* Lanham, MD: Rowman & Littlefield, 2003.

———. *Innocent Denied: A Guide to Preventing Sexual Misconduct by Teachers and Coaches.* Lanham, MD: Rowman & Littlefield, 2006.

Gates, Bill, and Melinda Gates. Speech given at the National Education Summit on High Schools, February 26, 2005. Available online at www.gatesfoundation.org/media-center/speeches/2005/02/bill-gates-2005-national-education-summit. Accessed March 21, 2013.

Hohenadel, Kristin. "Please Won't You Be My Inspiration." *New York Times*, March 18, 2012.

Hu, Winnie. "Bullying Law Puts New Jersey Schools on Spot." *New York Times*, August 31 2011, pp. 1, 23A. Available online at http://www.nytimes.com/2011/08/31/nyregion/bully-ing-law-puts-new-jersey-schools-on-spot.html?pagewanted=all&_r=0. Accessed March 21, 2013.

Hurst, Marianne D. "Columbine High: Five Years Later." *Education Week*, April 14, 2004. Available online at www.edweek.org/ewstory.cfm?slug=31columbine.h23. Accessed January 6, 2012.

Johnson, Jean, and Jon Rochkind. "Can I Get a Little Advice Here?" Public Agenda, March 2010. Available online at www.publicagenda.org/files/can-i-get-a-little-advice-here.pdf. Accessed March 21, 2013.

LinkedIn.com. Online discussion by members of the School Counselor Network group. Accessed March 15, 2012.

———. Online discussion by members of the School Counselor Network group. Accessed April 1, 2012.

Lloyd, Carol. "One R-Rated Movie You Might Want Your Child to See." *Great Schools.* www.greatschools.org/parenting/bullying/6317-bullying-school-movie.gs. Accessed March 21, 2013.

National Association of Secondary School Principals (NASSP). "Executive Summary of Break Ranks II: Strategies for Leading High School Reform." *NASSP*, 2004, pp. 1–6. Available online at www.nassp.org/portals/0/content/47560.pdf. Accessed March 21, 2013.

Perera-Diltz, Dilani M., and Kimberly L. Mason. "Ideal to Real: Duties Performed by School Counselors." *Journal of School Counseling* 6, no. 26 (2008).

Putnam, Robert D. *Bowling Alone.* New York: Simon & Schuster, 2000.

Reese, Shelly. "The Counselors Conundrum: Provide Triage or Full Service Program." *Middle Ground*, October 1998.

Rogers, Fred. *Life's Journeys According to Mister Rogers.* New York: Hyperion, 2005.

Sander, Thomas H., and Robert D. Putnam. "Rebuilding the Stock of Social Capital." *The School Administrator* 8, vol. 56 (September 1999). Available online at www.aasa.org/SchoolAdministratorArticle.aspx?id=14624. Accessed March 21, 2013.

Sinclair, Robert L., and Ward J. Ghory. "Last Thing First: Realizing Equity by Improving Conditions for Marginal Students." In *Access to Knowledge: An Agenda for the Nation's Schools*, ed. John Goodlad and Pamela Keating. New York: College Entrance Examination Board, 1990.

Texas School Counselor Association. "True North: Charting the Course to College and Career Readiness." National Office of School Counseling Advocacy, February 11, 2013. Available online at www.txca.org/images/Conference/SCC/13/handouts/Martin.pdf. Accessed March 21, 2013.

U.S. Department of Education. "The Three Myths of High School Reform: Secretary Arne Duncan Remarks at the College Board AP Conference." July 15, 2010. www.ed.gov/news/speeches/three-myths-high-school-reform-secretary-arne-duncans-remarks-college-board-ap-confere. Accessed March 21, 2013.

Whiston, Susan. "Response to the Past, Present, and Future of School Counseling: Some Issues." *Professional School Counseling* 5, no. 3 (February 2002): 148–55.

Winter Greg. "Wooing of Guidance Counselors Is Raising Profiles and Eyebrows." *New York Times*, July 8, 2004. Available online at www.nytimes.com/2004/07/08/education/08perks.html. Accessed March 21, 2013.

Zuboff, Shoshana, and James Maxmin. *The Support Economy: Why Corporations Are Failing Individuals and the Next Episode of Capitalism*. New York: Viking, 2002.

www.ingramcontent.com/pod-product-compliance
Lightning Source LLC
Chambersburg PA
CBHW062042270326
41929CB00014B/2507